Constructing a Nervous System

Also by Margo Jefferson

Negroland
On Michael Jackson

Constructing a Nervous System

A Memoir

MARGO JEFFERSON

GRANTA

Granta Publications, 12 Addison Avenue, London W11 4QR

First published in Great Britain by Granta Books, 2022
First published in the United States by Pantheon Books,
a division of Penguin Random House LLC, New York, in 2022

Owing to limitations of space, permission to reprint
previously published material appears on page 197.

A CIP catalogue record for this book is
available from the British Library.

1 3 5 7 9 10 8 6 4 2

ISBN 978 1 78378 554 4 (hardback)
ISBN 978 1 78378 900 9 (trade paperback)
ISBN 978 1 78378 421 9 (ebook)

Composed by North Market Street Graphics Lancaster, Pennsylvania
Offset by Avon DataSet Ltd, Alcester, Warwickshire

Designed by Michael Collica

Printed and bound by CPI Group (UK) Ltd, Croydon, CR0 4YY

www.granta.com

For Elizabeth Kendall and Charlotte Carter

Constructing a Nervous System

I

I stood in a bright, harsh light. The stage was bare.

I extended my arm—no, flung, hurled it out—pointed an accusatory finger, then turned to an unseen audience and declared,

THIS IS THE WOMAN WITH ONLY ONE CHILDHOOD.

It was part of the night's dream work. And I was rattled when I woke up, for I'd been addressing myself. My tone was harsh and my outstretched arm with its accusing finger had the force of that moment in melodrama when the villain (hitherto successful in his schemes to ruin the heroine's life) is revealed, condemned and readied for punishment.

I understood what I had to do.

At the end of his stage show, Bill Bojangles Robinson would look up at the lighting booth and shout, Give me a light. My Color.

Pause. Then

Blackout.

—

When the light returned, I knew it was time to construct another nervous system.

For most of my adult life I'd felt that to become a person of complex and stirring character, a person (as I put it) of "inner consequence," I must break myself into pieces—hammer, saw, chisel away at the unworthy parts—then rebuild. It was laborious. Like stone masonry.

And on the stone masonry model the human self says *go on.* Admires itself for saying *go on,* and proceeds to . . . *Go On.*

As I went on, I grew dissatisfied. This edifice was too fixed. I wanted it to become an apparatus of mobile parts. Parts that fuse, burst, fracture, cluster, hurtle and drift. I wanted to hear its continuous thrum. THRUM go the materials of my life. Chosen, imposed, inherited, made up. I imagined it as a nervous system. But not the standard biological one. It was an assemblage. My nervous system is my structure of recombinant thoughts, memories, feelings, sensations and *words.*

Repeat After ME:

It's time to construct another nervous system

—

You write criticism. You write memoir.

What will be your tactics, strategies, instruments for constructing this nervous system?

I keep carping and fussing, rearing up against the words "critic" and "criticism." Such august, temperate words. They make me think Gertrude Stein was right, that nouns are boring because all they do is name things, "and just naming names is alright when you want to call a roll but is it good for anything else." When you're thrilled by a taffeta petticoat, a flying buttress, a sound chamber of notes and syllables—when an idea makes you feel "as if the top of your head were being taken off"—then abandon your too-temperate prose zone and keep writing criticism.

As for "memoir," I keep attaching adjectives to it. Cultural memoir, temperamental memoir: What makes me so anxious? I want memoir and criticism to merge. Can they? And if so, how?

Read on.

There's no escaping the primal stuff of memory and experience. Dramatize it, analyze it, amend it accidentally, remake it intentionally.

Call it temperamental autobiography.

—

Be a critic of your own prose past. These words for instance.

A young novelist asked me: Why did you choose to write criticism?

I wanted to make my way to the center of American culture, and find ways to de-center it, I told her.

Why did you choose to write memoir? she asked.

I wanted to make my way to my own American center and find language for the fractures there, I answered.

These words aren't wrong, and they've worked to set the mood for readings. They're too smooth, though, too graciously incantatory. Too designed to show the valiant journey, the honorable aim. The rule assigned and assumed. (Stand up especially straight, please, you are one of the first black/woman critics here, you are among the first of your race and gender to steadily publish reviews in a cluster of widely read periodicals from the 1970s into the twenty-first century.) Writing to honor and claim a permanent place for the arts and cultures of non-white non-males and non-heterosexuals; writing to savor and display your ease with them all, including the arts and cultures of white male heterosexuals. Writing to display your own gifts and skills.

Is this commemoratively grand? Tonally accurate, though: those times and those settings required touches of self-protective grandeur. You were always calculating—not always well—how to achieve; succeed as a symbol, and a self.

Remember: Memoir is your present negotiating with versions of your past for a future you're willing to show up in.

. . .

On a stage filled with bodies, the adult orphans speak the last lines of the family play.

Exeunt alone.

Prepare to enter a new play.

As I write this I worry that I'm about to hurl raw intimacies at new, uncommitted readers. If I delay, though, I'm coddling myself. And pretending it's for their benefit.

2018: To My Mother

Dearest Irma,

You died four years ago. But the process of your dying continues. I domesticate it as best I can. I don't feel Romaine Brooks–ish now that you're actually dead. In my bleak, sere days I would whisper or silently intone her dreadful words—"My dead mother gets between me and life. I speak as she desires. I act as she commands." I didn't often add the last words, "To me she is the root enemy of all things." I'd memorized them but you weren't the root enemy—I was. You were crucial source material for my self-imposed deprivations.

I must have feared your judgment of the world I was making. Of what in it wasn't part of the world you'd curated for me with such meticulous and invincible ardor.

Why did you stop talking to anyone in your last year? You had not lost your mind. And when you could still speak, why did you refuse to answer when I asked you if you thought about Denise? Your oldest child, my only sister. I'd just asked if you thought about your mother: you whispered yes. Your mother had been dead for more than sixty years. Denise had been dead for only three. So you turned your face to the wall. Refused to share your grief with me. "My first-born," you'd murmured, when I told you she was dying. Maybe you were returning to the private life you'd shared with Denise for those first three years. As the prime intruder on that intimacy, my presence was not required.

You should have died before I had to witness your full descent. No speech. No movement except for your bladder leaking into your diapers. Refusing, even when you still had words, to share your death with me.

"We are continually bobbing and slipping out of the way of our would be re-possessors."

Amelia Etta Johnson, *The Nations from a New Point of View,* 1903

These re-possessors become our own griefs and quarrels.

Margo Jefferson, *The Psyche from a New Point of View*

I've misquoted Mrs. Johnson. Willfully, insistently misquoted her, ever since I read and copied out these words at least five years ago. This indefatigable Race Woman wrote "repressers," not "re-possessors"; repressers as in vindictive white people eager to subdue black people by force. Why—even when I reread the original passage—did my cognitive skills insist on turning "repressers" into "re-possessors"? "Re-possessors" had a sharper note of menace, of ruthless conquest, of violence done to others, then taken in and done to oneself. A final death in a family will make a nervous system go dystopian.

. . .

Death rouses the big emotions. But they have to adapt to the small scale of ordinary life—a life "unromantic as **Monday morning**, *when all who have work wake with the consciousness that they must rise and betake themselves* *thereto."* Your workaday monsters are grief and anger. Whatever's at hand—inconvenience, grudge, vexation—they rise and betake themselves.*

*Charlotte Brontë, *Shirley*

Supple, wily Monster of Mine:

You wait for one of those mornings when I've slept badly and wake up thinking ill of myself in a fretful way.

I go to the kitchen. I can't find the mug I want. I go to the bathroom. The container with my sterilized cotton balls is stuck. I'm furious: What did Carmen do when she came to clean yesterday—did she break the mug and not tell me? How did she close the container so tightly I may have to take a screwdriver to it?

I'm seized by a thought:

If I were a white slave mistress, this is the moment I'd call her into my presence, rail, slap her, throw an object—maybe the container—at her and warn her she'd be whipped if it happened again.

If I were a high-handed white woman in New York City, I'd chastise her sharply the next time she came here. If I were angry enough, maybe I'd fire her.

If I were a high-handed woman of color—black, brown or beige—I would do the same thing. And decide to hire a white cleaning woman so I could feel less guilty about my tone.

I get the container open with no screwdriver and no damage to my nails. It had probably tightened when Carmen polished it. I find the mug, which I'd left in the dishwasher, instead of in the cabinet with other mugs.

If I'd called Carmen and spoken sharply to her, would I apologize now? On the phone or in person? If I apologized, would she stay on? I know she needs the work. How would we proceed? Would we perform our old cordialities or adapt slightly—she more distant or more anxiously obliging, I more distant or more strenuously gracious?

Monster says, We're done with that. Let's move on. Today's clearly a day for you to feel blocked and impeded, a coward in work and love; resenting duty; suspecting pleasure. My job is to make sure you don't hold just anyone or anything responsible for your state of mind. You're an orphan now. It's time to blame your dead parents, and to do so properly you must be more nuanced. You must be literary.

Monster prompts me with a quote from the wise and balanced Willa Cather.

"Always in every family there is this double life . . . secret and passionate and intense . . . Always in her mind, each member is escaping, running away, trying to break the net which circumstance and her own affections have woven around her . . ."

I need my own variations.

"My dead mother gets between me and life." You've said that already, says Monster. Don't be repetitive. Your emotions repeat themselves but your allusions shouldn't.

"Daddy, Daddy you bastard, I'm through."

Sylvia Plath is overused, says Monster.

My parents enthralled me. My mother's ubiquitous charm, my father's artful dignity—they enthralled me.

Monster says: Your mother didn't love you enough to want you less than perfect.

Monster says: Your father didn't love you enough to prefer you to his depression.

Monster says: You've worked hard, you've left your mark. Maybe it's time to die. You're past the prime you wasted so much of. Why don't you join your parents? Imagine their faces as you walk toward them. They'll cry out, "Oh Margo, we're so happy to see you!"

Then I realize . . . that if any of this were possible—this Sunday School afterlife—they would be furious. My mother would cry: *How dare you waste your talents and achievements like this? All our work!* My father would look at me in silence, unutterably disappointed by this failure of honor and character.

And they would join arms, turn their backs and walk slowly away holding their heads high.

. . .

NOW IT'S TIME TO EMBRACE GRIEF'S INEVITABLE, SOMETIMES USEFUL BIPOLAR SWING!

I offer "No Good Daughter Now," after Ethel Waters's "No Man's Mamma," recorded in 1925 to a cheeky, joyous thirty-two-bar tune.

Waters Verses

I can say what I like, I can do what I like,
I'm a gal who is on a matrimonial strike.
Heigh ho! I'm no man's mamma now!

I can smile, I can wink, I can go take a drink,
And I don't have to worry what my husband will
think
Because, I'm no man's mamma now!

. . .

Jefferson Verses

I can say what I like, I can do what I like,
I'm a girl who is on a matriarchal strike.
Heigh ho! I'm no good daughter now!

I can sulk, I can pout, I can flounder about,
And I don't have to fear her judgment will flout
My will—I'm no good daughter now!

Exeunt Exuberant
The Orphan's Pledge

No more sweetly obliging chatter.
No more offerings of well-balanced cheer.
No hasty wardrobe adjustments to preempt critique.
Gone, compliance and resistance.
Assertion and submission.
Adoration and derision.
Can these binaries be undone?
No, but they can be done over. Repurposed.

. . .

It's time to renovate your psyche's domicile. It's been looking pretty shabby.

Look through your materials. Find ways to make them new or good as new.

Movie Clip from *I Am a Fugitive from a Chain Gang*
Starring Paul Muni, who played criminals and
crime victims with equal gusto in '30s Hollywood

How do you live, asks the woman who still loves the escaped and fleeing prisoner.

And Paul Muni calls back as his face slips into the black dark:

. . . I STEAL . . .

I steal too. I call it outsourcing. The text does part of the writer's contractual work: emotional, associative, intellectual, historical.

I imbibe these lines, that passage, those phrases to get the necessary work done.

I steal. I gobble. I bask in those moments when I am a fugitive from the confines of my own words.

Sometimes I amend the words of others. Always we converse. They people my solitude, shift its parameters. They hold the past, and they open into a space where nothing disappears or remains just what it was. Am I a parasite? Yes, but a benign one. I feed on words I need. And I give them new forms of sustainability.

Do I betray their original intent? I may. I do. When you were first learning to read, you stowed yourself away inside each new word, learned its contours, and then stood up, stretched your limbs and took it with you into the world.

I consume, I commandeer and stockpile these lines. They give me courage as I pursue dissonance, contradiction; fissures in and around this entity I call a self, a writer.

. . .

"True to oneself! Which Self? Which of my many—well, really that's what it looks like coming to—hundreds of selves? For what with complexes and repressions and reactions and vibrations and reflections, there are moments when I feel I am nothing but the small clerk of some hotel without a proprietor, who has all his work cut out to enter the names and hand the keys to the wilful guests . . ."

Katherine Mansfield, 1920

One of these selves is an aging self. This aging self notes that writers, especially women, are taking the subject up, trying new ways around and through its legacy of the cruel, the maudlin, the stoic, the grieving, the defiant. I'll have a few skirmishes with this aging business, starting with friends, ending with myself.

One friend is a great beauty, of whom people say (their relief at being younger sharpening their appreciation): "You can *see* she was a great beauty. She's still very good-looking." She's aware of this, and responds with a running narrative of her inner life as it adapts to her new circumstances.

The first time I slept with a man half my age, to the complete satisfaction of neither of us, I dreamed I'd stopped by my ex-husband's house on the way to the hardware store. He welcomed me warmly and we sat down for tea. But as I began to speak I noticed that the room was filled—crawling with, draped with, littered and encrusted with—nubile and languid young women. They were part of the wallpaper. They undulated slightly and made soft moans from time to time. Brian, I said, who are these creatures and why are they here? I wish I could say, he answered ruefully. I'm doing just what I always did and here they are.

VIZ. (in other words, namely)

Another great beauty who has crossed the border into "wonderfully attractive" spent the weekend with her thirty-year-old son and his thirty-year-old girlfriend, then reported:

I was a bit low when I got home. What would make me happy?, I asked myself. Annie growing older would make me happy. Not ill or infirm. Just older. I felt like Jimmy Stewart in Vertigo, *entreating Kim Novak to dress up as his dead wife: "Please, Judy. It couldn't matter to you!"*

VIZ.

I took growing pride in my toned body as I grew older, and in how well I worked out at my gym.

I got compliments regularly. Regularly attached was the archly hesitant question: "Do you mind if I ask how old you are?" One afternoon (it was the year I turned fifty-two), a nice-looking woman whom I gauged to be in her thirties approached me, waited respectfully till I'd put down my two twenty-pound kettlebells, then offered the usual compliment and the usual question. When I answered, she widened her eyes and brought one hand to the mouth she had let fall open. "My god," she said, "I thought you were much younger. I thought you were about forty-four." I'd been sure she wouldn't put me above forty and I was hoping for the last of the thirties.

I steadied my face and picked up my kettlebells. I was chagrined and ashamed. Twenty years later I still am. I was in compensation overdrive. And that young woman had punished me for it.

When men approached to praise me, they didn't ask about age unless they were trainers, explaining that my age was useful data for their work with older clients.

When they wanted to hit on me, they knew better than to ask.

Older women's tales—"Une femme d'un certain âge" tales—are hard to pull off. They risk being arch. I'll never renounce the pleasures the feminine has always given me: its materials, its histories, its small rituals and grand designs.

. . .

SIDEBAR

And yet, since my teens, I've avidly (often secretly) collected black male performers as alter egos. I admired, I longed to possess their styles. To wield them.

They absorb me still. With boldness or with stealth, these men placed themselves at the center of American cultural desires: they made themselves essential makers and players, even when that culture was doing all it could to maim, contain or expel them.

My fascination with black male performers was like a personal ad running through my head.

They're singers usually and they know how to move, gesture, give tension to stillness. If I were placing that personal ad, it would read:

> *Black Woman Seeks to interpret styles of black manliness culled from mid-twentieth-century arts and performance archives. (Peak years: the 1920s through the 1970s.) Please send examples. She values sonic and kinesthetic skills developed through calculation, innovation and selective mimicry. She envies men their aura of presentational license.*

It's not that I rate singers above instrumentalists, it's that singers satisfy my need to *voice* sensations, attitudes and emotions outside my gender performance range.

My models have included:

Gentlemen-Dandies of jazz and cabaret (Baritones preferred, e.g., Billy Eckstine, Johnny Hartman, Bobby Short, Andy Bey)

They built kingdoms of tonal and linguistic artifice: words stretched out, sunning themselves in the musical line; consonants slyly dropped then restored without a backward glance; timbres plush and plangent.

I cherished the masculine codes of diction: their artifice and syllabic opulence; phrases that croon, hurl forward and lightly brush; notes operatically flung up and laconically stretched out. Voices and manners that insinuate and insist, hint at rapture while maintaining a certain *noli me tangere* distance.

We loved them for the dangers they had passed.
We loved them that they showed no scars thereof

We loved the lavish fabrics of their singing.

Nat Cole: the protective perfection of vicuña; Billy Eckstine: silk velvet even when he knows it's a tad too plush for the occasion; Johnny Hartman: brocade with a subtly ornate texture; Bobby Short: a fine wool tux with impeccable trimmings—the black or polka dot bow tie, the red or white boutonniere. Andy Bey: a hand-woven sweater, dense and multi-hued.

Ike Turner, A Case Study: The Sociopathology of a Rhythm and Blues Man. Talent scout and musician, bringing Delta blues titans to avid record producers; a songwriter whose "Rocket 88" helped launch rock and roll; the Pygmalion-tyrant who launched potent Tina Turner; pushed and beat her till she fled, then remade both of them: her as a superstar, him as a disgrace.

MIXTAPE:
From "Sweet Rough Man," 1928
From "Daddy," 1965
I woke up this mornin', my head was sore as a boil,
And I said I do I do
My man beat me last night with five feet of copper coil
So daddy, I'm finally through.

Must I be stranded between Gertrude Rainey and Sylvia Plath?

No. I can't truthfully say "Mon semblable, ma soeur" to either woman. What I recognize here is the lure, the immersive lure of danger and dominance; of erotic and emotional cruelty tirelessly plotted and staged.

Aesthetic Indications of the Black Bipolar in Soul and Funk: Marvin Gaye and Sly Stone, church-raised youths precocious and ambitious. Tormented and drug-bedeviled by the 1970s. Listen to Marvin Gaye as his falsetto grows ever more haunted, spectral, each song a PTSD fever dream. Listen to the liquid screams and *Exorcist* growls of Sly Stone, his raspy patter and loopy scatting making each song into an associative talking cure.

Does the race I share with these men shield me from the taint of white culture's longue-durée obsession with black male bodies and psyches? Its predatory appropriation of black male styles? Its fixed binaries of pleasure/danger, love/theft, catharsis/cathexis?

When I like men I want to be like them . . . —I want to lose the outer qualities that give me my individuality and be like them. I don't want the man, I want to absorb into myself all the qualities that make him attractive and leave him out.

F. Scott Fitzgerald

These words must be from his notebooks. I found them in an old notebook of mine and they feel akin to what I'm doing. Imitating, explicating—and yes, plundering—to access powers my upbringing denied me.

Autobiographical narratives? Let me work my way there. Let me start from the shelter of a narrative "We." Call it a prologue.

Throughout our history, we black Americans have had to embody grand themes and ideas to gain white society's attention and support.

Justice.

Freedom.

Struggle.

The destiny of a people.

The destiny of our people was tracked through the male line. (We know the drill: across racial boundaries big ideas and themes have always been assigned to men. Women have been reinforcements, distractions, affects and justifications.)

Here's a discomfiting question. How long did it take the average black woman of my generation to become fully aware that we too had been lynched? It took me till college (1964–68) or just after (early '70s). If I'd heard or read this fact earlier, it had not sunk in. Yet according to historian Crystal N. Feimster, *between 1880 and 1930, close to 200 women were murdered by lynch mobs in the American South.* That's quite a knowledge time gap. I was taught to honor the many black women who fought (lobbied, protested, organized) against lynching. But that made us ancillaries, not martyrs and sufferers.

True, we had been raped. For centuries. And yes, that crime was unceasingly denounced and lamented: by our men and by us. Somehow, though, the language of lament and denunciation made the rape as much a crime against them as against us. Black men had been deprived of their right to possess and protect the most compelling symbol of success besides money: women whose value as unstained Ideals was universally agreed upon. Women who brought the men who'd won them impeccable social and sexual dowries.

So here I was, growing up just past the century's midpoint. I belonged to a race ruled lesser. I belonged to a sex ruled lesser despite its much-touted compensations. And I belonged to a subgroup of that sex—black women—that was ruled lesser still, even when we cadged some of these compensations. I craved imaginative compensations. License. I wanted to play in private with styles and personae deemed beyond my range. Beyond the laws, rituals and behaviors I'd been taught to live by. Live with.

Remapping, resettling American culture. Devising new modes and manners. Making art, making entertainment, making art and entertainment one.

Negro Men. Black Men.
I idolized them.

And now to another story, one told by an unsheltered "I." No plural here, no "we" for camouflage. What did this "I" do and what did she crave?

II

1957–59

I stare at the album cover: BUD POWELL: JAZZ ORIGINAL.

When I'm alone I take it out of the record cabinet and stare, whether or not I intend to play it. Sometimes I put it back unplayed. And think on that face, that dark, sweating face.

The camera has presumed to walk up and stare. He's closed his eyes. His face is shadow and smoky light against a gray & muted-black night expanse. His hair and mustache are black. There's a patch of white shirt and striped tie, a patch of suit. He could be floating alone in a cosmos of his own design. His lips are parted. (Humming, breathing as he sweats.) He's possessed by his music. In a state of ecstatic—let us use the Greek word for sweat: *diaphoresis.*

I was eight, I was nine, and I'd learned to slip the record from its jacket, hold it by the edges and avoid breathing quickly when I placed it on the spindle and pressed ("don't hit, press") PLAY. I would choose records for the whole family to hear, but I'd always find separate time to listen alone on the living room couch, sometimes rocking back and forth. When I played Bud Powell's records, I thought his piano was like Ariadne's maze, fingers winding into runs, angling into chords, lucidity racing virtuosity across every beat and turn. I was reading Greek myths then. I made him Theseus, of course, the hero wresting beauty and harmony from a monster's grasp, his right hand unspooling the red thread of coherence, left hand scrutinizing, probing, assessing his progress.

I couldn't admit, not yet, that he was the Minotaur too, half man half bull and of sacred origin; despised, feared, locked up and turned into a ravenous monster whose task was to kill the young and beautifully human. Bud Powell was a genius-monster, made a genius through hour on hour of ravenous music listening and practice; made a monster by years of cop beatings, medications, liquor, breakdowns, electroshock treatments, heroin and forced confinements in mental institutions. Half man, half beast—the designation assigned blacks and enforced by law and practice. The punitive ire of rulers who imprisoned them in institutional labyrinths where their task was to destroy themselves and thereby demonstrate their own inherent debasement. The famous story, the legend: Powell, playing the piano keys he had drawn on the wall of one such place, asking a visitor, "What do you think of these chords?" Don't pity him. He'd crafted the tool he needed to flee brick and concrete for the glass enclosures of his music.

Brave monster, lead the way!

Give us headlong runs; give us cheeky headstrong chords and titles. “So Sorry, Please.” “Tempus Fugit.” “Un Poco Loco”!

Then suddenly my preteen heart would crave the more buoyant strains of romance. And I’d turn to Erroll Garner. He was bold and virtuosic. He and Bud Powell were peers. But his temperament was merry and exuberant.

The evening breeze caressed the trees . . . Tenderly.

I loved Erroll Garner’s version of “Tenderly.”

It was written as a waltz the year I was born, a waltz of flowing upward lifts and downward sweeps; even when jazz musicians made it a 4/4 ballad they kept its mood of suave rapture.

Erroll Garner bestowed that rapture. His piano led you into the abandon of postwar Romance. He was a buoyant, lavish sybarite.

Powell’s wary notes withhold the lilt and ache of the song’s opening, letting (or making) us find our way to the melody, pausing to let notes that seem about to become impetuous almost stutter; withholding, testing runs and letting us have a few measures of rapturous dynamics, chords “kissed”—here they’re almost battered—“by sea and mist . . . Tenderly." A few quiet treble runs, self-contained arpeggios and a dissenting interval.

Impossibly elegant ("Parisian Thoroughfare"), he slays the monster and triumphs. No, he's still the monster, an impossibly elegant monster, a brave monster, defying with his harsh left-hand chords, his right hand probing, constructing, sometimes repeating those emphatic beats in measure after measure like a willfully aggressive speech pattern. Don't pity him.

"Strictly Confidential," suave and cheeky: Harlem nonchalance.

My father had told me a bit about Bud Powell. The musicians he awed night after night at Minton's on 118th Street. (Now, as I write, I'm playing "In Walked Bud"—Monk based it on the chord changes of "Blue Skies.") In walked Bud and scattered particles of light became skies of boundless blue. He was a genius, my father said. He went mad. I heard it as he blazed through unsanctioned notes and chords. What was it like to blaze and blast through unsanctioned states of mind? This was not encouraged in my father's family. Doctors, lawyers, judges, teachers: all were guardians of sanctioned honor. Of the exemplary, which was closely bound to the sacrificial. My father always spoke gravely of our menaced and martyred race giants. He'd begin by talking to me—I felt respected—and he'd end staring into a silence where the weight of elegies, past, passing or to come, was his alone.

"If it were possible, [I] would gather my race into my arms and fly far away with them." Years later when I read those words of Ida B. Wells, I almost dropped to my knees. She could have written them for my father. He'd longed to be a jazz musician, not a doctor. He'd played the trombone and he'd worshipped Duke Ellington. Oh to be what Lawrence Brown was, the Duke's chosen trombonist. To heal with art.

Why did you choose pediatrics? I once asked him.

I wanted to find out what was wrong with people who couldn't tell me themselves, he said.

He wanted to be a rescuer. He became one.

But more, he wanted to be rescued.

He struggled—fought, gave in to, resisted—depression all his adult life. Though it was not referred to as such in our home. He was sitting in the den, thinking and reading his medical journals. He was listening to music. He was napping because he was tired after hospital rounds and house calls. He was tired, I'm sure, after the daily, monthly, yearly work of being an exemplary colleague, a loyal friend, a benevolent and responsible provider. After a lifetime of racist incidents and intrusions, despite and amid his achievements.

They could enrage me, these valorous, wounded men.

Gentlemen-citizens, mastering the arts of rectitude and sacrifice. I was a child. I was a daughter. Why did I have to absorb all this?

Why couldn't Bud Powell find a way to be Theseus—slay the monster, defy the men who'd made him one, and outwit the monster inside himself?

Why couldn't my father find time to gather me in his arms each day and take solace in my company?

He took pride in my brightness, my school successes, the talent my piano teacher Muriel Rose said she saw in me. (Miss Rose had studied with Florence Price, the first Negro woman to have a symphony performed by a major symphony orchestra. The Chicago Symphony Orchestra.) Miss Rose had been a composer before she became a teacher. What sacrifice, what quiet martyrdom lay here? Had she abandoned composing as my father had abandoned his trombone?

Maybe he hadn't wanted children—he was already caring for so many. But maybe having no children would hurt a pediatrician's credibility . . . So even if he didn't want them, he might have felt he needed them for professional reasons.

In his later years my father wept every Christmas when he opened his gifts in the living room or heard a choir singing "The Lord's Prayer" or "The Hallelujah Chorus." He wept and then he began his own recitatif of racial injuries and exclusions, some oft-told, some newly declaimed that morning.

—The marching band he was not allowed to join at the University of Southern California. The white directors let him join the regular band. He was a good trombonist, they said. But the marching band was a university spectacle meant to affirm the easy, unconstrained unity of athletes, fans, families and donors. A Negro in their midst would mar the symmetrical patterning of this whole.

—The black classmate, a music student, who was not allowed to join the school orchestra: early one morning he sneaked into the chapel and began to play the organ, insistently, masterfully . . .

Awed students paused, listened, whispered: Who could that be?

The chords swept through the chapel doors and out into the campus, holding dominion over all.

My father put his head in his hands. It was so beautiful, he cried and wept.

One Christmas morning, after we'd opened all our gifts, he stood in the kitchen doorway wearing his new robe as Mother prepared our ritual breakfast—sausages, baked apples, biscuits. It was 1989. A new decade beckoned. He locked arms with my sister and me. Talk of the past began innocently, benignly—Midnight Mass at St. Edmund's, Maggie and John's raucous holiday parties—

when Daddy stopped. His eyes veered past us. He began the plunge into a scourge-and-shame race tale.

Mother was impatient. Affronted by this lockdown of memories they'd acquired to savor together.

—Ronald, why do you always talk about the bad things? They were so long ago. Why can't you remember—and here, like a dutiful and resentful child caught making a fuss and feeling shamed, he gave a small laugh. *Why can't you remember the good things?* he chimed in to parrot and placate her. Then, pausing to let the good things shrivel before our eyes, he wheeled around and turned his back on us.

It Was a Bitter Dose, he said. A Bitter Dose.

I did not follow when he left the room. There would be time enough to inherit his despair and shape it to my own ends. To name it, acknowledge and not deny it. To wrest it, as best I could, from the stigma of racial weakness and failure: counter the shame it caused so many black people. To make it a necessary part of one's quest to be "a person of inner consequence."

The nine-year-old I was decided: I should not have to take all of this in. I will turn these confounding dangers, these losses, into what I can manage: scenarios to follow; reactions to memorize and absorb; a workbook of behaviors. Preventive pedagogy. I will quash what's unbearable. It's a Long Playing Record to be returned to the cabinet.

. . .

I've reached an emotional stalemate here. I want to dilute, possibly delete this "ah the lifelong wounds of childhood" climax. I feel a little ashamed.

"Sometimes it is better to be a little ashamed rather than silent." (Czeslaw Milosz)

Should I turn around and take us back to adult life?
No. Let's stay where we were.

I put the Bud Powell record back in the cabinet.
I take out an Ella Fitzgerald record . . .

On her album covers Ella Fitzgerald dresses tastefully. On the cover of *Ella Sings Gershwin* (1955) she wears chic nightclub attire: a ranch mink stole beneath which we glimpse a dusky rose gown in a fabric shimmering discreetly. No lurid outsized jewelry. On *Ella Sings the Duke Ellington Songbook* (1957) she wears a smart black middy blouse with a white sailor collar and white cuffs. Her left hand holds sheet music; a sleek lady's wristwatch and gold wedding band are also visible. She is as much matron as musician.

On a spinning black disc she sounds like all I could dream of: she's a romantic comedy heroine with perfect pitch and varied pace. Mischief, longing, quicksilver charm.

In the 1980s when my best friend (white) is writing about '30s romantic comedies I play at a game of appropriation and compensation; I match her white Hollywood stars with MY black jazz ones: Ella is Jean Arthur and Carole Lombard; Ivie Anderson is Claudette Colbert; Billie Holiday is Barbara Stanwyck.

The black disc is spinning through the late 1950s and early '60s, back to my preteen-girl state. Like most preteen girls I long to be physically desirable; like most black preteen girls I long to be physically desirable while also being physically impeccable. Her tastefulness does not make me enjoy looking at Ella Fitzgerald's album covers. She is portly. Forever portly. The first lady of jazz never sheds pounds dramatically, never transforms herself against all metabolic odds to sashay across the set in for-flaunting outfits. The way Judy Garland does. The way Oprah Winfrey will.

She can't lose weight. And when she sings on television . . . she sweats.

—

Black women of achievement and ambition with ambitions need to be wary about their public relationship to sweat. (If you're Althea Gibson or Wilma Rudolph, barnstorming your way to tennis or track glory, it's understood that you must sweat to succeed. But don't bring it out of the locker room.) Historically, sweat is for workers who have no choice but to labor *by the sweat of their brows, the sweat in their armpits, the sweat that soaks through their clothing, making it stained and smelly.* "Work and sweat, cry and sweat, pray and sweat!"

Ella Fitzgerald sweats on TV, in concert halls, in nightclubs (are there sweat stains on that dusky rose gown when she's through performing in it?), on national television shows. On television sweat dots her brow and drips, even pours down her cheeks. Sweat dampens her pressed and curled hair. Sweat runs into the stones of her dangling earrings. Like Louis Armstrong, she uses a white handkerchief. Louis Armstrong, Satchmo the Great, dares to sweat before multitudes. He knows many of his white fans think it's happy sweat. Smile and sweat, laugh and sweat, play music, sweat! Onstage and on television he's never without his white handkerchief, wiping the sweat from his face, wiping the spit and sweat from his trumpet valve. His African mask of a face (the beaming-grimace smile, the fixed popped eyes) makes this a ritual, though, not a necessity. His ritual of artistic diaphoresis.

Who makes fun of his girth, his dark skin, in public? HE wipes his sweat vigorously, proudly; SHE dabs at hers quickly, almost daintily. If a woman *dabs* at sweat it becomes more feminine, more refined. It gentrifies into euphemism; it becomes "perspiration," the provenance of ladies, not indelicate working-class women. But on television white women singers do not ever sweat and they barely perspire. Ella Fitzgerald does both. Which means that, even as she swings, scats and soars, Ella Fitzgerald's sweat threatens to drag her back into the maw of working-class black female labor.

To her years on the streets, alleys and sidewalks of New York: to age fifteen when her mother dies of a heart attack and her stepfather gets abusive, when she flees to an aunt in Harlem, then to the streets of Harlem. The once-excellent student cuts school day after day.

Does courier duty for a numbers racket.

Does lookout duty for a brothel.

Earns small change with bits of song and dance.

Gets arrested.

The charge is truancy and the courts dispatch her to the Colored Orphan Asylum in Riverdale, New York. Why is she sent upstate to a reform school a few months later? Who has she angered? What has she done? Is this asylum—the only one in New York to house colored children—overcrowded?

Ella Jane Fitzgerald is sent to the New York State Training School for Girls in Hudson, New York, a reform school for white and black girls, and the only such racially integrated institution. Seven of the ten the judge sentences that year are black. Most of the inmates, whatever their race, have been convicted of nothing but truancy.

> truant (noun) means "beggar, vagabond"; truant (adjective) "wretched, miserable, of low caste"; truanting (verb) means "escaping, rebelling, despairing, despising, raging in perpetual motion."

All of these girls, thirteen to fifteen years old, arrive bearing the weight of terms like "wayward," "morally impaired" and "incorrigible." Ella, in the words of the judge, is "ungovernable and will not obey the just and lawful commands of her mother." Thank you for your careful attention to this case, Judge. Her mother is dead.

Once they arrive, the girls are housed in squalid cottages and often—we can assume regularly—abused in various ways by the staff. This would be the place to note with rue that at least there was a choir for Ella to sing with. There wasn't. Only white girls were allowed in that choir.

She is, however, singled out for solo beatings in a locked basement.

A year later she makes her escape. By what means? Does someone help her? A girl pal with her own plans to escape? A sympathetic cook or janitor who leaves the basement door unlocked?

She walks, runs, crawls, hitchhikes the 112 miles from Hudson, New York, to Harlem.

Over valleys, streets and alleys, winding trails,

Over highways, rocky byways, through hills and vales . . .
(Ethel Waters, "Lonesome Swallow")

She is making her bid for whatever self-governance the streets will allow. Scuffle, shuffle, warble; stand outside the doors of nightclubs and theaters (or squeeze your way in to listen); do what you must with whoever pays you something for a night's bed and board. You will wrassle up a future or join the anonymous thousands who live and die trying.

At last it's 1934! At last it's time for this seventeen-year-old runaway to walk onto the stage of the Apollo Theater, and into her destiny as the Swing Muse of Harlem. She will win its fabled Amateur Night contest; she will be noticed, introduced to important bandleaders. But she's still the brown-skinned girl in the raggedy clothes: Fletcher Henderson won't hire her. What about Chick Webb, the bandleader whose drums rule the revels at the Savoy Ballroom? He must be persuaded to; she's too ugly, he protests the first time around—he of the hunched back, the tubercular spine that will kill him five years from now. Does he worry that the sight of two plain people onstage, one malformed, one gawky and chubby, will presume too much on the goodwill of his merry-making audience? But he's persuaded. And rewarded. Three years later Ella is responsible for the band's first nationwide Number One hit record, "A-Tisket, A-Tasket." The words and tune are hers, as is the idea. *It was a game I played in the orphanage,* she says lightly, and says no more.

I started to brood about this in 1996. Every December *The New York Times Magazine* does a tribute issue for the celebrated who'd died that year; I was asked to write about Ella Fitzgerald. I wrote: "Ever since I found out about the horrors of Ella Fitzgerald's youth I've wanted to protect her from the scrutiny of critics and fans like myself, who have always inflected the pleasure we took in her singing with patronization. Sweet Ella, we said when she was alive, she's wonderful but she has no emotional depth. Poor Ella, we say now; she did suffer but she denied it—banished it from her life so she could dwell in a pristine musical wonderland."

May 1938

She is twenty-one.

From her mother's love untimely ripped, she tucks an elegy into a nursery rhyme.

The standard nineteenth-century version

A-Tisket A-Tasket / A green and yellow basket

I sent a letter to my love and on the way I dropped it.

Ella's 1938 version

"A tisket, A tasket, the *wrong*-colored basket!" jokes *New York Post* columnist Earl Wilson, for Ella has made the song's green and yellow basket brown and yellow. But how could brown be the wrong color for brown-skinned Temperance Fitzgerald who left Newport News, Virginia, with her daughter Ella Jane circa 1920 and settled in Yonkers, New York, where a better life could be sought and found.

I sent a letter to my love / And on the way I dropped it.

Ella sends her letter to the mother she lost at fifteen, the emblematic mother of those fairy tales she must have read in her Yonkers elementary school, the mother of Cinderella, and Snow White, who dies too young to shield her daughter from cruelty and neglect. (Ella's voice curls into near–baby talk when she sings the word "Mommie.")

The Original

I dropped it, I dropped it
And on the way I dropped it
A little boy he picked it up
And put it in his pocket.—

Ella makes the thieving boy—a "little girlie" like herself—a gleeful doppelgänger, who goes "trucking on down the avenue" (make it Lenox Avenue), who goes "peck-peck-pecking all around / Until she spies it on the ground." (As Chick Webb's drums voice Lindy Hop's chicken moves,) Ella's double steals the letter without missing a beat.

Abandon hope all ye who enter the sphere of a child's despair.

She took it, she took, she took my yellow basket
And if she doesn't bring it back I think that I will die!

It's a child's wail kept in check by the implacable, impeccable beat. The orchestra's a congenial but watchful guardian; on the good behavior of a snappy riff and major key.

Which Ella Jane rejects with a minor key retort and a defiant unresolved note. Do not deny a child her despair.

If that girlie don't return it
Don't know what I'll do!

Here's the point I suddenly realize—she's becoming the song's auteur. Coding, shaping her future as a soloist, a band member, a leader and collaborator.

It's a stringent discipline even when it's ebullient and joyous.

The band indulges her with eight bars of major-minor call-and-response. When her voice curves around the beat, heading for a lament, their chorus keeps her firmly upright and up-tempo.

Oh gee, I wonder where that basket can be . . .
So Do WE So Do WE So Do WE So Do WE
So Do We!

Oh gee, I wish that little girl I could see.
So do We So do We So do WE so do We
So do We!

The legato balm of saxes will sweeten her next outburst.

Oh why was I so careless with that basket of mine?
That itty-bitty basket was a joy of mine.

But "itty-bitty basket" is a baby girl's plaint. If she'd been a perfect child, her mother might not have died.

Futile to mourn, says the band. You're a grown girl now. You're an errand girl for rhythm. Pulse. Syncopate.

A TISKET! (March!) A TASKET! (Yes!)
I lost my yellow basket!
Won't someone help me find my basket
And make me happy again a-a-gain?

Ella slips a quick blue note into that last triplet.

The band supplies a few minor key measures and then

they all hit the playground for a jaunty call-and-response finale.

Was it red?
NoNoNOOONo
Was it green?
NoNoNOOONo
Was it blue
NoNoNOOONo (with a growl on that third NOOO
to fully expel those blue days)
Just a little yellow basket!

A snappy four-beat salute from the band, a snappy retort from the singer . . .

The record spins to an end and hurtles up the music charts.

TOP OF THE WORLD, MA! This twenty-one-year-old orphan is a star who will live and flourish for fifty-eight more years, securing her reign as the First Lady of Song and the First Lady of Jazz. And for fifty-eight years she will not speak of her past. Ever. She will offer no pained or ruefully tranquil admissions, no touchingly unguarded confessions. She will refuse our scrutiny and our pity.

I know nothing of this when I take Ella Fitzgerald LPs out of the record cabinet at age nine, seeking a pristine musical wonderland. It's her sweat and her heft that give me intimations of a black female destiny she has thwarted. It's a destiny that every hour, day and year of my young life is plotted to prevent. The crucial plot elements are: an irrefutably fine education; excellent (when possible, perfect) manners and grooming; a thoroughgoing exposure to the arts; an outgoing personality; a figure well suited to stylish clothes; a face that doesn't flagrantly violate Nordic beauty standards. In this swathed and sheltered life, I am squeamish about the public evidence of her sweat and size.

In 1994 I review Stuart Nicholson's biography of She Whom We All Call Ella. And I find this excruciating item from a 1938 issue of *Downbeat* magazine. "220 pounds of songstress" goes the headline, then: "Portly Ella Fitzgerald was a bit late for a recording date last week when she was caught in the escape hatch of an elevator. The infernal machine stalled between floors and Ella, already late for a recording date, endeavored to escape through a trapdoor in the top of the cage. It took three strong men to rescue the 220-pound songbird. Ella opens March 28 at The Blue Note."

I want to beat them around the head and ears till they cry Uncle and beg her pardon.

Do ardent fans of the 1950s and '60s, when her status is assured as the First Lady of two music realms, politely call her "big" or do they just go ahead and call her fat?

(Not without pity—it's such a lovely voice, they quickly add.) Do fans of all races and nations do this?

Are her black fans more courteous than her white ones? Whatever their race, however much they respect her musicianship, do her male musicians talk this way? Do they joke that she probably started sweating even more once she entered menopause? Not to her face, no, but behind her back, when she can't control them with her ravishing, diaphoretic musicianship?

Always she dresses with alert matronly care, always the right outfit for club, concert, TV or record studio appearances. Earrings meant to be distinctive without being show-offy. A slender gold lady's wristwatch. Sometimes a semi-natural cap of frizzy curls—that was in the '50s, and how contemporary and smart, how unashamed it looks now. (The young singer Camille Thurman said she watched all of the videos, feeling such pride, taking such pleasure in Ella's appearance, which she found inseparable from her music performances.) Ella was never at ease with TV show patter, staged spontaneities; she'd clasp her hands in her lap and gesture a bit uncomfortably after the retort, the rehearsed reaction to a joke. When she'd sing, though, she'd unselfconsciously cup one hand to one ear so as to hear herself at work.

—

Ella Fitzgerald, your mind was your music laboratory, stocked with elements to be broken down and recombined. Melodic and harmonic phrases, inserted, interpolated; digressions and decoys. You worked hard for your sweat. You earned it like Bud Powell, like Louis Armstrong. And here I can't stop Yeats from entering my head—those lines from "Adam's Curse" where the male poet labors to make beauty and the female muse labors to be Beauty. I can't stop them from entering my head, but I can stop them from doing the same work they did in college, when I first read this poem.

Ella Fitzgerald Rehearses

I said, "A line will take us hours maybe;
Yet if it does not seem a moment's thought,
Our stitching and unstitching has been naught.

Ella Fitzgerald Flees Caste Servitude for Music Service

Better go down upon your marrow-bones
And scrub a kitchen pavement, or break stones
Like an old pauper in all kinds of weather;

Ella Fitzgerald Claims Her Artistry

For to articulate sweet sounds together
Is to work harder than all these . . ."

Ella Fitzgerald knew what every woman ever belittled, ignored, dismissed or penalized for being not-beautiful knows in her beauty-pauper bones.

"To be born woman is to know—
Although they do not talk of it at school—
That we must labour to be beautiful."

At the end of your 1960s Berlin concert you took hold of that sweet and lovely standard "How High the Moon" and built it anew as an explosive eight-minute swing-bop expedition into popular music archives, "popular" by now including Charlie Parker, Ferde Grofé, Harold Arlen, Slam Stewart, Rimsky-Korsakov and her own "Tisket." Parenthetical phrases, melodic digressions, harmonic insertions—it would be profligate if its proportions weren't flawless. At critic Will Friedwald's last count, you drew on forty-five compositions for your extended, mostly scatted solo. You end with the opening lines of "Smoke Gets in Your Eyes," that resplendent Kern and Harbach love elegy.

"They asked me how I knew / My true love was true," you proclaim, like a bugler sounding a wake-up call.

"I of course replied, / Something here inside" —And then "cannot be denied," that languishing next line, explodes into an ebullient "SWEAT GETS IN MY EYES"!!!

After that it's easy, it's just a matter of scanning an octave and letting the final four "Moon"s take off like the four stages of a rocket.

Ella Fitzgerald, you labored to be beautiful.

You earned your diaphoresis, day by day, night by night, rehearsal by rehearsal, tour by tour.

People should have begged for the elixir of your sweat every step of the way.

I do.

I beg for it.

You made your way to the center of American culture. You made your own musical language. You turned the maw of black female labor into the wonderland of black female art.

III

with our lacks
“We work ~~in the dark~~—we do what we can—we give what we have.”
Henry James, “The Middle Years,” altered

We look for expedient muses.

My memory is not stocked with sumptuous sensory data, a profusion of image and metaphor. When I feel thwarted by this—when it feels sparse rather than spare, in my memory book I think back to a certain spring afternoon in 1996.

It was late April. I was walking on Manhattan’s East Side, near Sotheby’s auction house, when I saw a black man placing a sheet of cardboard on a street corner near a parking meter. He moved with steady care, smoothing the corrugated edges so that they lay flat on the pavement. Then he put two clean Styrofoam cups in the center, placed a clear plastic cup that held straws behind them and laid a set of white plastic cutlery in front. Still moving carefully he shaped six deli napkins into a fan, which he placed to the left of the fork. Finally he propped a hand-lettered sign against the meter, put his Styrofoam contributions cup beside it and sat down, cross-legged, his hands on his knees.

The sign read:

Choice Selections from the Jacqueline Onassis Auction

That's when I remembered that Sotheby's was conducting theirs a few feet away.

O black and unknown bard! I murmured, quoting the James Weldon Johnson sonnet.

He had produced a rarefied domestic space for public viewing, an improbably canny version of the feminine art Mrs. Onassis was renowned for, just as its relics were being avidly purchased by monied admirers.

He had also produced a gloss on Zora Neale Hurston's "Characteristic of Negro Expression." He was not only "decorating a decoration," as she wrote: he was decorating a deprivation.

Lesson from the Sotheby's bard: A writer works with what she lacks as well as what she has. (Watch a dancer adapt a movement to the constraints—the particular length and flexibility—of their limbs. Listen to an actor or singer shift a line's rhythm to fit their range and timbre.) Assess your lacks to see what use they might be put to. Develop other sources of plenty.

Ask: What do I want desperately to write and how shall I write it? What am I trying not to write? When do my fluencies become clever distractions from what needs writing? How often have I watched with acute irritation a performer's distractions, hissing silently, "Why don't you stop making that step, that melody easier than it is? Why don't you find another way, another technique to get at it? Take the risk that it won't have the same affect you so admire and covet in some other artist. (That supple arabesque, that quietly sustained high note.) All right. You can't get that longed-for effect by the same means. Have at it in another way! Can an unexpected tension in the line, a surreptitious harshness in that note make it work?"

And so, back to my memory bank's relatively low stock of sumptuous sensory data, its ready stock of tainted data. My sensibility is a structure of recombinant thoughts, memories, feelings, sensations and words. It syncs concord and discord, trying not to simplify them. It lets gaps and distortions remain.

I'll decorate the available decorations.

I'll decorate the deprivations.

Gone with the Wind

The first time Denise and I read *Gone with the Wind*, we were thrilled. Avid readers, both of us. Too young to be discerning. I'd push our ages back to seven and ten if I thought I could get away with it, but I think we were nine and twelve.

Why was the paperback in our house anyway? Our mother must have read it. I know she saw the movie. I remember the gusto with which she once described how she'd like to end a dispute she was mired in: "I'll draw myself up with a coolly dismissive air and say, 'Frankly, my dear, I don't *give* a damn.' "

Yes. In 1940, she and her friends had gone to their all-black South Side neighborhood theater to see the notorious *GWTW* despite the full-throated denunciations of the Negro press, not least their own *Chicago Defender*.

As enlightened young Negro women they surely knew better.

As avid consumers of female glamour they knew what they wanted.

They wanted to study its tropes and lures, whatever the context. Choose which ones to adapt, and which to mock with confidence. They were in their twenties. Civil rights lobbying—pressure here, pleading there—had gotten the word "nigger" removed from the script. The word "darky" remained, as did a brief slightly coded allusion to Rhett Butler's KKK alliance. These enlightened young Negro women were old enough to know this fact: their race would never win most of the battles and skirmishes they entered.

Pleasure was a privilege they were entitled to as compensation. Performative pleasure was a way of taking what a culture had to offer and making it your own without asking for permission.

Was their behavior also a case of "nose-to-the-glass syndrome," in which—across an invisible yet implacable barrier—the excluded turn their gaze raptly on the beautiful and powerful, memorizing their ways, longing to playact in their dreamscape? I won't pretend this kind of longing was absent. But I think theirs was a prideful choice too, compensatory but prideful: a choice to be frivolous and lighthearted. Shrug off caste constraints. Walk through the glass and succeed at playing the beautiful, powerful ones.

So these enlightened young women chose to repurpose Scarlett's "fiddle-dee-dee!!" (Not pert and high-voiced but wry and elongated, with an accent on one or both "dees.") They appropriated her flirty willfulness to use in flirtations of their own. They adored Clark Gable's Rhett—Scarlett certainly needed chastening, like so many spoiled white women, and they identified with him each time he put her in her place. Still, they appreciated her feminine determination to win him back. And Vivien Leigh's being British supplied a welcome distancing effect.

The one tangible reward—so tangible, so debatable—offered to the Negro public was Hattie McDaniel's Oscar nomination for playing Mammy, the type of the dialect-driven antebellum slave who'd cleaned, cooked, dressed, advised, scrutinized and strategized for generations of white heroines; the Mammy young black women had been taught they were fortunate to be better than (let's rephrase that—"fortunate to have more opportunities and skills and natural attributes than"); the Mammy at the service of heroines they'd been taught they were as good as but would never be treated as well as. The first Academy Award nomination for our race. Advance or set-back? Both. Spur to pride or contempt? Both.

On Academy Award night, the factotums of MGM placed a resplendent McDaniel (wearing "a tasteful rhinestone-studded aqua evening gown, white ermine jacket and a bountiful corsage of white gardenias") at a small side table in the Cocoanut Grove so that she would not be close to the audience of applauding peers whose physical distance from her ensured their professional appreciation of her. Fay Bainter prefaced the announcement of her name with the oleaginous assurance that "the entire nation will stand and salute the presentation of this plaque." Hattie McDaniel had prepared her own remarks. She managed to leave those MGM had prepared for her at the table. She walked purposefully, in fact she strode to the podium.

"I sincerely hope that I shall always be a credit to my race and to the motion picture industry," she said, accepting the award. What American Negro did not harbor a private version of that first hope? "My heart is too full to express just how I feel," she said, weeping. What American Negro did not understand the emotions contending in her heart as she left the stage? The Negro press reported that, at the after-party, Vivien Leigh kissed her cheek and Clark Gable shook her hand.

Cautious participation; ongoing denigration: these were the tracks laid down for The Negro by the glittering machinery of American entertainment.

Come the 1950s, as Denise and I read *Gone with the Wind* we were able to detach ourselves from Margaret Mitchell's Mammy, her high-voiced factotum Prissy and the barefooted, pigtailed children ("pickaninnies") who darted on and off the page. They were so removed from the world we inhabited that we used our reading habits to turn them into folktale figures. Like garrulous peasant women, and village busybodies, like bossy mothers with foolish daughters. We did our best to seal their grotesqueries into long-ago stories from faraway lands.

But now the movie overtakes the book in my shame-tinged memory: I can only see Mammy, Prissy and the other slaves onscreen. MGM re-released *GWTW* in theaters three times between 1954 and 1961: When did Denise and I persuade our mother to let us see it? Were we seven and ten, ten and thirteen or thirteen and sixteen? (When we could have gone by ourselves.) So my account of how Denise and I coped—by denial, disguised as the frivolity our mother had practiced twenty years earlier—is (again) a movie account.

Again, Denise and I did our best to sever ourselves from *Hattie McDaniel's* Mammy, from *Butterfly McQueen's* Prissy and from the unidentified Negro children in slave tot garb. Our best wasn't good enough. Prissy's giddy babbling was an affront—we scorned her. We mocked Butterfly McQueen's name too—though I now know that she'd acquired it for her youthful performance as a Butterfly in a *Midsummer Night's Dream* ballet.

Hattie McDaniel's Mammy rattled us. Her girth and loudness, her dialect-slinging bossiness were an embarrassment, and normally, embarrassment would birth condescension. But Mammy wasn't just bossy, she was forceful. She was knowing. And she feared nothing.

We feared so many things, Denise and I. We knew they were lesser things. They didn't belong to the world of slavery. They belonged to the world of cautious privilege-parsing equality. We needed some part of Mammy's fearlessness. But her caste-bound presence was useless in our world. Useless and possibly humiliating. Whenever white privilege-parsers looked at us, they could choose to see her.

What happens when you're a viewer, spectator, reader who craves imaginative adventure and has no—I don't want to say models, I'll say avatars—to conduct identity experiments with and on? I hate the position this threatens to put me in—the position of one who is desperate and abject, heir to the racial curse of self-doubt and self-hatred. I like to claim *there's power in learning to imagine what hasn't, can't and won't imagine you.* What kind of power is it, though? Negative capability won't suffice—too much of white art requires a negative capability that negates whole parts of one's self. Maybe it's like learning a language that's simultaneously dead and living, that requires you to amend it even as you absorb it. You must never deny how much you wanted it. You must never deny what delights it gave you. You must never disguise how punishing it could be. You must never deny how much and just what it cost you. In that collaborative consciousness lies your power. And your pleasure.

I felt good about these words for some time after I wrote them. Then one night I decided to rifle through an old file box of index cards filled with quotes I'd copied down years before. And there was one from Condoleezza Rice. No date, but clearly from the Bush Jr. presidency years, 2001 to 2009, when she was often asked to describe her close working bond with the commander in chief.

"It's not my influence over him," I'd recorded her saying.

"I'm internalizing his world."

Stricken, I closed the file box. This cast an ominous light on my oft-stated belief that there is strength to be gained from imagining what hasn't the will, skill or wish to imagine you.

"I'm internalizing his world . . . I'm internalizing his world." . . . The words echoed and stretched themselves out in my head. My vision wavered, like those movie moments that signal a traumatic flashback.

I was periodically obsessed with Condi in the Bush years. So were most of my black women friends. She was One of Ours. Far more powerful, more famous and more ethically dubious, but built, trained and launched by our own black bourgeoisie: a product of its ferocious love and labor. As secretary of state, she made global policy decisions, she gave practical orders, she controlled life and death in a world as morally skewed as antebellum Tara.

Attached to the note card was a folded piece of paper on which I'd typed a passage from her 2012 autobiography, *Condoleezza Rice: A Memoir of My Extraordinary, Ordinary Family and Me* (nowhere to be found on my bookshelves now. I gave or threw it away). That passage read—let's put it in boldface:

"My parents had me absolutely convinced that you may not be able to have a hamburger at Woolworth's, but you can be President of the United States." (p. 41)

And when you discover you can't, you become a kind of cyborg, a confidante and extension of a president you can be intellectually superior to and emotionally in thrall to—or at least enthralled by.

My righteousness was going into tonal overdrive. I knew it had a touch of the phobic. Was a variant of "ma semblable, ma soeur" angst being churned up? Time and again I'd been smitten by white male American icons against my better taste and judgment. My icons were entertainers, though, show people. Imagining and internalizing their world was like an after-hours excursion to an off-limits neighborhood. It was a pastime, not an ideology.

Take my long-standing obsession with Bing Crosby.

That's right. Bing Crosby.

Mr. White Jazz, Mr. White Christmas, Mr. record/film/radio and television star from the late twenties to the late seventies; singing "Basin Street Blues" with Louis Armstrong; singing "The Little Drummer Boy" with David Bowie; Mr. high-jinks prankster on the road from Hong Kong to Zanzibar with Bob Hope; Mr. country-western patriarch, pledging fealty to the "Dear Hearts and Gentle People" of small-town America.

I'm Bing Crosby

America first sees me as a Paul Whiteman Rhythm Boy frolicking in the fields of jazz, shooting the breeze with Bix and Louis, learning from them, slipping, sliding, plunging into the musical phrasings of black jazz, slipping out again, to become CROSBY THE CROONER, luring love songs into my vocal chamber, plying them with baritone liquids and tenor-trilled jewels . . . Der Bingele (the one and only). In me, the lustrous and the fatuous walk hand in hand.

I am a smooth and honeyed purveyor of ballads that could have been penned in the parlors of eminent Victorians.

Where the blue of the night meets the gold of the day
Someone waits for me-e-ee.

Youth fades. Business opportunities arise, as do cultural responsibilities. I embody the pristine, priest-clad dreams of a nation. I give my people *Going My Way* and *The Bells of St. Mary's*. I am a multi-millionaire with shares in the Santa Anita racetrack. Eventually I launch my own racetrack. Eventually I have seventy-five golf club memberships.

The tarbrush sound of my youth is a trick now, a wink-wink titillation for festive occasions.

Watch me at Newport in *High Society.*

Fooling around with Satchmo: "Now You Has Jazz/ Jazz/Jazz Jazz JAZZ!"

Swanning around with Grace Kelly: "I give to you and you give to me, True Love, True Love . . ."

I love the early Bing.

I am in thrall to the later one.

So I have made *Mis*ter Crosby my personal minstrel man.

Everybody needs a minstrel man and black women like me have finally won the right to ours.

Oprah had Dr. Phil.

Condi had George Bush.

I have Bing Crosby.

Rules for minstrels:

—They must do something in public you want and aren't allowed to do. Dr. Phil for instance: he never smiled or made warm little jokes. Dr. Phil never worried about his hair. Dr. Phil never handed out presents. Dr. Phil snapped out advice in his Texas twang, and let those supplicants know sympathy would cease if they didn't shape up.

George Bush didn't have to be stringently self-possessed. He didn't have to be grammatically correct. He didn't have to demonstrate every day in every way that he was truly outstanding and truly deserved the rewards routinely given him.

Bing Crosby can act however he chooses—suave, naughty, pious, feckless—and win acclaim for it.

Minstrels must have some performative essence (gestural, verbal, behavioral) that you (spectator, imitator and opposite) hold in contempt even as you crave its license. The minstrel's behavior attracts and repels you. Such willfulness! Such shamelessness! Such presumption! You long for that performative license but you've been taught it's unworthy. Inappropriate. You have higher standards and better values. You're sure of that. But if, however briefly, you could act like that . . . get away with it . . . be rewarded for it . . .

I'm Bing Crosby now. I'm easy. I'm golden. Bad things happen to some reasonably good people around me. They don't happen to me. When my wife Dixie pulled me out of alcoholism then fell into it herself and floated there until dead, I gave an Oscar-nominated performance as an alcoholic three years later. When two of my four undistinguished sons killed themselves . . . WHAT COULD I DO?

I have my work and my golf. I'm impeccably amiable for the public but I **have my moods** and they need attending to by those who live or work with me and for me. When I walk into the recording studio with my hat tilted to one side you know I'm feeling good; ready to shoot the breeze. If my hat is on straight, do not attempt pleasantries. Do not address me at all.

I'm Bing Crosby.

I can get away with anything.

I'm entitled to everything.

And if you question what motives drive these white minstrel mergers and acquisitions of mine, here's a scene from fifty-seven years ago, when I got stuck as the comic target in a Bing and the Boys routine. Call it *Road to Raceland.*

It was a sunny June night in 1964. I had just graduated from high school and was cutting my swath through a party given by a classmate (white). A boy (white) I'd never met walked up to me and said with an insinuating smile, "Hi. I see you're a Negro. Brian told me you were." I reared back doing whatever a sixteen-year-old girl's version of sputtering was. Then I strode off and took shelter among the girls (white). It was presumptuous, condescending, I declared. It was, they concurred soothingly.

A few minutes later, my classmate-host appeared. He was known as a jester and his smile was merry. Was I really offended, he asked, eyes sparkling behind his glasses. His friend had just meant to convey solidarity, he felt he'd earned the right to speak that way because he'd gone down south for the civil rights demonstrations. Had I gone yet? he queried with calculated innocence.

If I produced a reply, I have no idea what it was. Clearly it didn't suffice. Call it another example of Post-Mortification Memory Disorder.

Fifty-seven years on I still go over that first exchange and fume. Exactly what had so rattled and offended me? It began with that stranger's "I see." So breezy. So fatuous. So . . . gratuitous.

Gratuitous. That's the clue. At those convivial, largely white parties, race difference was supposed to be gratuitous. We were friends, peers, classmates; we were comfortable in our mise en scène likeness. This "I see" ruptured my mise en scène credibility.

And how presumptuous the words that followed. *"I see you're a Negro. Brian told me you were."* Race as behind-the-back gossip. With what added tidbits about my looks and personality?

He was bantering—it was a tease and a flirt-opener. But race made it a power move I couldn't abide. I see you're a Negro. It shows I see both your lures and your liabilities. They're inseparable and I like that. I find you attractive. I find the struggles of your people interesting. They're worth my attention. So are you. I want you to be excited by that. And I want you to be grateful for that.

As Louis Armstrong was supposed to be grateful to Bing Crosby, as all black entertainers in those years, decades and centuries were supposed to be grateful for the appreciation and sometime collaboration of white colleagues.

Etymology: *Like* **gratitude**, *grace and congratulate,* **gratuitous** *is a descendant of the Latin word* gratus, *which means "pleasing" or "***grateful***." When* **gratuitous** *was first used in the middle of the seventeenth century, it meant "free" or "given without return benefit or compensation." The extended meaning "done without good reason" or "unwarranted" came about just a few decades later . . .*

I was not going to be grateful for his racial and sexual gratuities.

IV

Don't think it's all cheeky reversals and appropriations, this making your way through American culture, having your way with it. It's a maw too, a mosh pit; it's whiplash and mimicry; it's flowery beds of ease laid over cursed ground and unquiet graves.

In 1969 I bought a frayed paperback edition of *Uncle Tom's Cabin* on one of the knockoff outdoor shelves at the Strand Book Store. I bought it expecting to sneer my way through its racial sophistries and female pieties. I was on a quest for women writers considered serious, "literary" despite being labeled minor or lesser. I was sure Mrs. Stowe wouldn't make the grade. But I begin to read anyway, and eventually, like Eliza crossing the ice, I found myself leaping from piety and sophistry to something much grander and landing, by means too varied and contradictory to recount, on the side of moral and narrative freedom.

I felt I had to wrest Harriet Beecher Stowe from the gender-tainted disdain of male critics (Henry James, James Baldwin), even as I punished her racial errors and corrected her cult-of-true-womanhood frailties. Baldwin had flung her from the canon of worthy literature. *Ain't I a woman?* That's part of why I chose not to.

I wrote interpretations of Stowe's characters, monologues, for Tom, the saintly slave and martyr; Topsy, the impish slave orphan; and Eva, the pure-of-heart Anglo-Saxon child. I called Adolph, that clever foppish house slave, American literature's first queer black man. (He primped, he pouted, he all but snapped and double-snapped.) When his master, Augustine St. Clare, died, Adolph was sold to a man whose gleeful harshness barely concealed sexual aggression. As for St. Clare, he was a dandy whose most aesthetically perfect creation was his child bride of a daughter, Eva.

I was obsessed with Tom and Topsy. They tried so—between and beneath Stowe's words—to get past the confines she'd built, as if they could sense the scorn generations of blacks would feel for them.

I rewrote Uncle Tom's death scene, marred in the book by his prayerful protestations of love for his torturers.

The beatings of his owner, Simon Legree, and the slaves Sambo and Quimbo left blisters, bloody scabs and pulverized flesh upon his body. He prayed for salvation, and saw instead a future in which his goodness—his unnatural piety—would make him an outcast, a traitor to his race. He turned to his maker, crying:

You wouldn't do this to me if I were a white man.

And Harriet Beecher Stowe, looking back on the wounds and hidden scars of her own life (punishing father, children dead or stillborn, ceaseless domestic labor), answered: I would if I could, Thomas. I would if I could. (To hold an Anglo-Saxon male in such thrall—not yet, not yet!)

I'm no Frederick Douglass, he said, I know that. I don't want to go north and write my memoirs. I don't need to act grand like Paul Robeson. But I died because I wouldn't reveal the escape plans of two slaves. Women slaves. Can't you do more with that? Why do I have to keep telling Legree I love him? Why can't you give me part of that speech you wrote at the end: ***"Not surer is the eternal law by which the millstone sinks in the ocean than that stronger law, by which cruelty shall bring on nations the wrath of Almighty God!"***

These were my lines, she said. You still speak Ebonics.

The Curse of Uncle Tom will fall on your head, he cried. Your people will be ashamed of you. You'll be held up to women as proof of their inferior gifts. You'll be patronized and disavowed by serious writers.

You'll wish I'd never been born.

Then the book closed over him.

He woke bound in black print and white.
Delivered into his readers' hands.

I was even more obsessed with Topsy, the outsider black girl, angry, anarchic and new—so new—to American fiction. Her closest relative is Hawthorne's dark-hued Pearl, the willful child of sexual sin's "rank luxuriance." Topsy is the child of racial sin, of slavery's rank viciousness. In Stowe's words, she represents "a class of slave children, quick, active, subtle and ingenious, apparently utterly devoid of principle and consciousness, keenly penetrating, by an instinct which exists in the childish mind, the degradation of their condition, and the utter hopelessness of rising above it . . ." To me she is the model of a furious abjection that has never ceased to haunt black women. A return of the repressed that they welcome and repurpose.

1852

"'How old are you, Topsy?' [asks Miss Ophelia, the sternly moral New Englander put in charge of her soul's redemption].

"'Dunno, missis,' said she, grinning like an ugly little black doll.

"'Don't know how old you are! Did nobody ever tell you? Who was your mother?'

"'Never had none,' said Topsy, with another grin.

"'Never had any mother! What do you mean? Where were you born?'

"'Never was born.'

"'You mustn't answer me like that, child,' said Miss Ophelia sternly. 'I am not playing with you. Tell me where you were born, and who your father and mother were.'

"'Never was born,' said Topsy again very decidedly. 'Never had no father, nor mother, nor nothin'!'"

(It's the fate of an abused child to speak truths that most adults can only bear to think of as fantasies.)

1853

Harriet Jacobs of North Carolina—a slave in fact, not fiction—has fled bondage after hiding in an attic for seven years. She is working in Boston as a nursemaid, and living in fear of fugitive slave catchers who prowl the city. She is struggling to write her own autobiography, rather than gifting it to Mrs. Stowe for anecdotal use in *A Key to Uncle Tom's Cabin.* Often, she is stricken by shame and grief, even a perverse longing for the solitude of her attic retreat: "the old dark cloud comes over me," the dark cloud of a past shaped by her master's sexual abuses and by her attempt to alleviate them through a sexual alliance with a more powerful white man. She cannot "write the life of a Heroine with no degradation associated with it . . ." But, as she labors to pull the story from its hiding place inside her, to turn anguish, bitterness and shame into persuasive abolitionist prose, she writes a white woman friend, confiding:

"I sometimes wish that I could fall into a Rip Van Winkle sleep and awake with the blest belief of that little Witch Topsy that I never was born . . ."

Topsy has become a household idol, a spirit to enact griefs that lie too deep for speech.

1994–2017

That little Witch Topsy is reanimated by the artist Kara Walker. She multiplies on canvas and paper, finding ways to give and get abuse. Topsy kills a chicken, sucks a penis, rides on the back of an aged Negro man, bends over to be anally fucked by an aging white man; drifts in space like a napping homunculus. Topsy reappears with a clean white sunbonnet neatly tied beneath her chin, a raised axe in the left hand, a severed white male head in the right, heels clicking together, lips flapping, eyes staring. Ceaseless work, this, but at the day's end she'll pose for her portrait, holding a succulent slice of watermelon, wearing a wide-brimmed straw hat and white bib apron with her name on it: TOPSY. There are small gold hoops in her ears (the same ones she stole from Eva in *Uncle Tom's Cabin*). Four braids protrude neatly from her head.

The protean black girl-child: a model of furious—antic—exuberant abjection. Harriet Beecher Stowe's Topsy became a Christian missionary in Africa. Kara Walker's Topsy knew better. When American horror has invented you, you stand your ground and invent it right back.

. . .

Injustice insists on its ancestral right of return. It's tenacious and versatile. It adapts to shifts of time place and character with plus ça change insouciance.

Lexington, Kentucky, late 1830s: "Captain Marryat complained that a gentleman could not rent a carriage on Sundays because slaves with ready money invariably rented them first for their own pleasure."

New York, New York, mid-1920s, *The Great Gatsby:* "As we crossed Blackwell's Island, a limousine passed us, driven by a white chauffeur, in which sat three modish negroes, two bucks and a girl. I laughed aloud as the yolks of their eyeballs rolled toward us in haughty rivalry.

" 'Anything can happen now that we've slid over this bridge,' I thought; 'anything at all.' "

Caste Reversal in Hyde Park–Kenwood, Chicago, c. 2000

When she turned eighty-five and decided to stop driving, my mother arranged for Vilma, the Lithuanian woman who cleaned her apartment each Saturday, to take her grocery shopping. How is that going? I asked a few weeks later. Her voice exuded satisfaction.

"Vilma reaches into the car so carefully," Mother told me. "She stretches her arms out and says, 'Let me help you, Mrs. Jefferson.'"

"And I place my hands in hers and think: Look who's driving Miss Daisy."

This is a retirement benefit. My mother doesn't abuse her power, not in what she pays Vilma, what she requires of her or how she acts toward her. She's earned this, after years in the race labor force. She has social security and social superiority now. Soon enough she'll be too old and sick to enjoy them.

Caste Chat between two Black friends in a restaurant near the Metropolitan Museum, 2020

D: I don't know why I keep saying "sorry" when I call the waiter over for something.

M: We were taught good manners, scrupulously and compensatorily.

D: That's a good way of putting it.

They resume eating.

Families model caste relations. Families imprint them at the most primal level.

A Writers' Conference, c. 2015

Over drinks the talk turns to childhood. One writer seizes the lead to declare:

My parents were much more interested in each other than in me. Some nights when they were dressing up to go out yet again I'd whisper: "I wish I'd never been born."

What I meant was: "YOU WISH I'd Never Been Born." I couldn't say it out loud, though. I couldn't risk one of them answering honestly.

The speaker was white, but her words brought a cruelly serene Akan proverb to mind. *One does not acquire a slave in order to be affronted by him.*

Its parental equivalent could be:

One does not produce a child in order to be disappointed by it.

Or worse still:

One does not produce a child in order to be bored by it.

One does not construct a self in order to be bored by it either. Move on, Narrator.

Stretch your range.

. . .

I am at the Art Institute of Chicago. I am standing in front of a painting with a friend I've known and loved—fought with, then loved again—since we were eleven and she signed her name in blue ink on the front of my red leather clutch bag and crossed it out in black ink two weeks later when we quarreled. We're in our twenties now. She's a Kohutian therapist; I'm a book reviewer. We're at the midpoint of the 1970s; we're two of the many young women plotting destinies and careers.

We're quiet now, in green-thought-green-shade mode as we gaze at *The Song of the Lark* by Jules Breton.

What is it about this large painting, which Willa Cather claimed as the title of her ecstatic 1915 tale of solitary female genius, yet had to assure readers she knew was "rather second-rate"; what is it about this painting by a nearly forgotten artist that even now stirs young women again and again? Why does it matter to us that in 1884 France, a youthful peasant girl on her way to work in the fields at early morning stops and looks up to listen to the song of a lark . . . Forgetting the harsh scythe in her hand, her dull brown skirt and rough white blouse, the blue cotton apron, the pale brown hair shut up in a scarf . . . She listens, lips parted, eyes skyward.

"The title was meant to suggest a young girl's awakening to something beautiful," Cather wrote, and she used that title to tell the story of a provincial girl, a Swedish peasant of the American Midwest—awakening to her own astounding gift for music.

Now, a good half century later, my friend and I study it. "This picture gave me my first sense that I could have a separate life, even though I was a twin," she said. A life away from ceaseless mergings and dispersals, shared intuitions and unshared thoughts.

This moves me. "I think it's even harder to live a life separate from a powerful older sister," I tell her. She rears back, and starts to laugh. "Margo, you're so competitive you could be a twin," she tells me. And my heart soars! For I'd never thought of myself as ardently competitive in that way. No: I strove to follow the counsel of my honorable father, I strove to compete only with my best, my higher self. What did I do when unquashable bolts of fear and envy seized hold of me? I did my best to redirect them toward longing. Toward Resignation. Toward Appreciation for the plentiful gifts of others.

What a revelation now, an awakening to a force I hadn't known I possessed. Competition had slipped across my threshold like an animal I'd thought too cunning and driven, too feral to thrive in my habitat. It had chosen me, found me worth its demands.

What was it about competition that so electrified me?

—

It was the letting go, not of scruples or ethics, but of cowardice. I was writing lucid, comely reviews, turning down or accepting then withdrawing from interesting assignments I'd decided were beyond my powers. Flaunting then concealing my depressive plunges, keeping friends attentive and worried; steadily rejecting lovers who were likely to stick around; periodically choosing ones who, by temperament or circumstance, were sure to be gone soon. If someone wanted something that I wanted too, I'd decide I should renounce it. They deserved it just as much. Maybe they weren't the point; I was. Unlucky. Handicapped. Tainted. (There were so many options.) And if I chose to compete, maybe all I might win was their enmity.

Twins were born to compete and commingle. Twins were in perpetual concord and dissent. I wanted that kinetic alliance inside myself. For my life and for my writing. Which meant I'd have to attune myself to competition's behavioral extremes, its calculated desperation. I needed to study my past for evidence that I could pull this off; I needed to write my own ethnography of competition.

. . .

Jump cut to 2017.

Jay Z is a star and Beyoncé is a galaxy.

"I'm Ike Turner, tune up baby, no I don't play," he blusters on her "Drunk in Love" hit.

"Now eat the cake, Anna Mae!"

Oh no you don't, I think. I knew Ike Turner before you were born. I knew him before you knew yourself.

I was thirteen years old when I first played Ike Turner in our living room. The year was 1961. "A Fool in Love" had been released the year before. I'd played the Ikettes to my sister's Tina. They had a mordant world-weary coldness when they warned Tina, "*You know you love him, you can't understand / Why he treats you like he do when he's such a good man.*" I tried to give a three-fates quality to this three-woman chorus while I watched Denise strut and punch her way into Tina's 4/4 Maenad rapture.

"I Think It's Gonna Work Out Fine" was a dialogue. This time Denise decreed that I would be Ike; it was my job to master his line readings.

Let's begin.

Tina's words are in italics; Ike's are in boldface.

Ike's introduction is a two-measure guitar riff. (It's gutbucket razzle-dazzle.)

—*Darlin . . .* Tina croons. (It's gutbucket crooning.)

—Yes Tina—(Ike's voice has the rule-the-roost affability of a '50s television dad.)

—*You start to getting next to me—*

—Honey that was My Plan from the very began. Between smooth folksiness ("Honey") and deliberate malapropism ("The very began"): he's toying with her.

—Darlin . . .

Addressed with this endearment, Ike's formal **"Yes Tina"** downgrades to **"Un hunh . . ."** Is he just preoccupied or is he starting to find her intrusive?

She's definitely pushing her luck in Verse 2. The diminutive nickname—

Ikie

elicits only a blasé

Um-hum

I went to see the preacher man—

That gets his attention. **The *Preach*-er Man! you must be losing your "MI-ii-nnd"** he exclaims, giving **"Preach"** an aggressive vaudeville punch and **"Mind"** a horror film quaver.

I started—

His curt **Started what?**—should warn her but she pushes on.

Started makin wedding plans. . . .

OH REEEEEELY?????

A bridge of doggedly repeated affirmations (an abused woman must keep finding ways to flatter her abuser into good spirits), and then with 1:20 minutes to go, Tina and the Ikettes push through to a happy ending.

Ike has nothing more to say. Let the little girl dance, he thinks. Let the little fool dream. Let the record hit Number 2 on the *Billboard* Hot R&B Sides chart. In retrospect, her last scream-shouts, well-pitched and well-placed though they be, sound desperate. (Given the years that lay ahead, they were not the last desperate sounds she was destined to make.)

"He wasn't my type," Tina would say years later. He was onstage at the Club Manhattan in East St. Louis. She was an eager ambitious young thing sitting in the audience. And when he picked up his guitar and started to play, the music knocked her out. "I thought God I wonder why so many women like him. He sure is ugly. But I kept listening and looking. I almost went into a trance just watching him."

Honey that was my plan from the very began. . . .

I was thirteen when I almost went into a trance playing Ike. Everything about him was impermissibly low-life. The pile-up of processed hair, the tight tight suit on the bone-thin frame, the pointed shoes. The long face. Impassive, sullen, watchful.

Physically I found him alienating—almost repulsive. And fascinating. Was it *the mere radiance of a foul soul*? Not altogether. It was his contained manipulation of his materials. He set the structure, the beat, the pace. He stood impassively before voracious crowds and bent them to his will, seeming indifferent all the while. Tina ravished. Tina thrilled. But if you were that thrilling, if you gave every gyrating limb and throbbing muscle to being thrilling, you risked . . . I was too young to know *what* you risked. ("Young and Dumb" to borrow the title of an Ike song.) What mattered most to me then was that other girls, starting with my sister, were better at being Tina.

They were the Chicago version of those "Rule-the-roost" girls in Tina's St. Louis high school, "all-black but very high-class," daughters of doctors, school principals and other professionals, who made her feel "sort of lower-class." Her mother was a maid; the man her mother lived with was a truck driver. "What I always wanted was the principal's daughters' world." And her role model, ne plus ultra, was Jacqueline Kennedy—a model she shared with plenty of those principal's daughters.

I considered leaving this passage about the "principal's daughters' world" out. I thought that in pointing up these class and style distinctions I was using irony more for self-regard than self-awareness. It feels necessary, though. There's such a fraught history—intellectual, political, artistic—of how the black bourgeoisie has used, honored, disdained, studied, learned (borrowed, stolen) from, been inspired by, gone slumming in—the culture of The People; The Folk. The girls in my world are anecdotal evidence. And we were right to want her talent and craft, even if we were too naïve and too snobby to call them that.

If I couldn't manage Tina, what about the more pert and diminutive black girl group leads—Ronnie Spector, Diana Ross, Gladys Horton? I practiced their gestures and attitudes. I mimicked their voices and facial expressions. At every club meeting, at every slumber party I went to, one or more of my black friends did them better.

I had an alternate dream life with the pale maidens of folk music. They sang as if bathed in light, their sopranos wafting over us. I wanted to possess the nonchalant moxie of a girl group singer and I wanted to be a limpid belle dame with a guitar. I could struggle for the first—practice my gestures, tones—but the second was out of my reach. I channeled my longings into the maidens. First the ones like Joan Baez and Judy Collins. They were extensions of those poets of preadolescence—Sara Teasdale, Elinor Wylie, Edna St. Vincent Millay. Their lyric gifts made them utterly desirable and utterly feminine. They did not move onstage, so their bodies, clothed in sweet and simple garb, were extensions of their voices and spirits. They still wore the outer garments of female purity, though they discarded them to be earthly love objects. The maidens had been or would soon be chosen by flashy male rebels like Dylan. The lesser ones shadowed their powerful lovers onstage, basking in being chosen, harmonizing in clear thin voices. Mimi Fariña led by Richard, Sylvia led by Ian, Jean led by Jim. However sexual they actually were, they all exuded something innocent and plaintive. Was it the Rapunzel hair, drifting past their shoulders and almost caressing their guitars? Was it that they were all sopranos and always white? But no, Joan Baez wasn't all white. And yet it never really signified that she was half Mexican. A person of some color, whose people included the illegal immigrants, the deportees she honored through Woody Guthrie's protest songs.

There was Odetta, oh yes—the black mentor and matriarch of the mostly white folk revival, and a symbol of its roots in a political protest that was black-inspired. But Odetta was ten years older than the other women and (as far as we knew) had no part in the sexual couplings and uncouplings of the revival's rising stars. I was too young and greedy for central casting femme glamour. Odetta's persona was stalwart and stoic: heroic in the Charles White or Elizabeth Catlett manner. I could admire her. I could be uplifted and stirred by her. I could not imitate her.

I needed a secret source of performative energy. And

I sensed that Ike, Impervious Implacable Ike, had something to offer me. Something I could use. Something about expecting to be pleased instead of working to please.

Like the tougher boys at black rec room parties—the boys with the moves and half smiles, who sauntered up to you and held out a casual hand to signal "let's dance," putting both arms around your waist and grinding into your stomach if it was a slow dance. If you didn't want to, you had to suck your abdomen in and push your butt out. Tricky that. None of them was menacing in the Ike mode. And some of them were sexy. But the rhythm, the pace, the structure were all theirs.

You had no style of choosing, only ways of being chosen; complying with pleasure or from duty, evading or resisting as artfully as you could.

I've chosen the plural "you" here because I want the adult feminist satisfaction of knowing I was not alone in those teen girl feelings.

Let it go, Margo. Each girl responded according to what she wanted, what she thought she should or shouldn't want, and what she thought she could or couldn't get.

Seductive, commanding black manliness and talent! Lucky Tina, to have the shiny glittery object of yourself to offer. You go to the East St. Louis nightclub where Ike leads the Kings of Rhythm. You wait for your chance to do . . . what? . . . Now Ike's onstage playing a B.B. King song you know . . . you seize the microphone your sister's boyfriend has offered her—and you start to sing. Your music blows the man away. He runs off the stage, grabs you and brings you right up there with him. "And I was in: I started singing with The Kings of Rhythm."

> Ike and I were like brother and sister. He went out and bought me my first stage clothes: sequined dresses, honey, in pink and silver and blue, with long gloves up to here and rings to wear over them. Bare-back shoes, the stockings with seams, even a fur stole . . . We would pull up to the club and I would get out and walk in and sit there real grand, like I was a star. And after a while, Ike would call me onstage. He'd say "Now we're gonna bring Little Ann up." And I'd walk up there and sing my three songs, and everybody would clap. It was wonderful.

One does not acquire a protégée in order to be overshadowed by her.

If she'd stayed Little Ann, instead of fulfilling her destiny as Tina, the name he'd given her to honor those white warrior-maidens, Nyoka the Jungle Girl and Sheena, Queen of the Jungle. If her success had foregrounded his instead of obscuring it. If she'd stayed as addicted to Ike as he was to cocaine . . .

Here's some backstage dialogue we teen girls were not privy to. (Or were some of us, in the privacy of our homes, when our parents fought, not caring if we heard or watched?)

Ike: What's on your fuckin' mind?

Tina: Nothing, Ike.

Ike: Yes it is. You're just tryin' to fuck with me.

And finally—*bam! Bam!* And then *Whomp! Pow!* And then the shoe would come off . . . and there I was. And then he would be fine, as if nothing had ever happened. And I'd be onstage *thrying' to thing* through these cut and swollen lips.

A black woman with a potent style always risked being downsized, turned on, by a black man who'd begun as an ally, mentor or lover. I once heard the bassist Curly Russell talking about Sarah Vaughan in the early bop years. She was out there improvising as hard as any of us, he said. *"We had to hold her back."* (Italics mine.)

I appropriate Ike Turner to sneer: "Oh *REEE-LY*?"

Don't you wish you'd had her talent, Mr. Curly Russell?

Don't you wish you'd rehabilitated your talent with the arduous razzle-dazzle your ex-wife did hers, Mr. Izear Luster Turner?

Even now when I see a video or hear an old hit, I'm drawn back in. He was an R&B man, a soul man, a pioneer rock and roll man. When he got to the crossroads, his soul was in thrall to manic depression and drug addiction; to years of envy (of Tina, of white rockers turned millionaire stars; of blues men he'd once helped sign to record labels—B.B. King, Bobby Bland, Howlin' Wolf all legends now and where was he?); to a Mississippi childhood that was a trifecta of domestic abuse, sexual treachery and racist violence.

"Remember?" Tina all but croons.

"Remember what?" comes his flat, hard response.

She presses on, determined to ingratiate.

"They used to call you Dapper Dan . . ."

The narcissism of nostalgia rewards her!

"Those were the good old days!" he crows.

"The thriller" she crows back—

"The KILLER honey" he corrects proudly—

"The ever-ready lovin' man!" she offers.

"That's me!" he chortles.

Ike Turner was born in 1931. His Baptist preacher father was an ever-ready loving man whose conquests included the girlfriend of Bird Dog, a white thug who came by the house one day and, with his henchmen, took Reverend Turner into the backyard and set about kicking holes in his stomach. "I remember it like it was yesterday," Ike said years later. "That door bustin open and Mama tryin to hold on to Daddy and to me, too, and them pushing her to the floor. For a kid in his mother's arms, it was a long way to fall, you know?"

A fall that could only be relieved when he recast and restaged it, the woman's jaw busting open as she falls to the floor; Ike dragging her across the room, kicking her in the stomach, standing tall over her prone body, then going about his business as if nothing had happened.

Remember?

Remember *what*?

Takin' Back My Name is what he called his 1999 autobiography. *Risin' with the Blues* is what he called his last (and first Grammy-winning) album, released in 2006, the year before cocaine, heart trouble and emphysema took his life. "I Don't Want Nobody" he rasped on one number:

I can do bad,
Can do bad all by myself.

—

"We didn't know then at the time, but he was bipolar," said Robbie Montgomery, an eight-year veteran of the Ikettes. "That's what they call it now. Back then we called it crazy."

Izear Luster Turner.

His foul radiance haunts me still.

. . . .

The same year Ike and Tina Turner had their first cross-race nationwide hit, four Negro girls crossed national borders and racial constraints to become gold medal Olympians.

Denise and I were always looking for ways to insert ourselves into tales of glory and glamour, especially when they starred Negroes. Sometimes it was a bidding war. Denise's three-year advantage gave her first dibs on Lena Horne; I bided my time and snatched Diahann Carroll. Denise did Imperious better. I did Exuberant better. Denise had longer, better-defined legs; I had a smaller waist and fuller breasts. Denise was statuesque. I was diminutive. We brought our uncertainties along, likewise our vanities. We told these tales through our needs.

THE BLACK FEMALE BODY

These days we boldly study the ways in which it was mocked, maimed, degraded. We honor the scars and fragments, we give them meaning. Restorative meaning. We investigate the black female body's present, consider its future possibilities.

THE BLACK FEMALE BODY

Resides now in the sanctum of historical analysis and artistic reinvention. We savor its revelations. We do not fear it.

But so many of us once did. Its public display, its interpretation by strangers or enemies, stirred unease and ambivalence—shame—in black women everywhere.

"Wilma Rudolph and the Tennessee Tigerbelles" Denise would shout all through the summer of 1960. She'd use her Al Benson DJ voice—streetcorner punch, back porch drawl—and I'd echo her as we cheered their Olympic track and field victories on TV (*exsultate jubilate!*) and followed news stories. (*Life* and *Time,* admiration; *Jet* and *Ebony,* exhilaration.) We ogled the magazine photos of Wilma's body in motion, crouching, launching, straining, elevating. Denise's legs were long, muscular and brown, like hers. But Denise was a dancer, and every week those forceful limbs of hers were being refined by ballet aesthetics.

Unadorned by dance technique, the athletic female body was an instrument of pure competitive skill and drive. Especially the black female body, which lacked stock footage of ideal feminine norms. It was thrilling to see the Tigerbelles in action on the track. To keep seeing them in photos became embarrassing.

That's how I remember it anyway, though research shows that my squeamish self-surveillance got certain things wrong. In fact, according to *Time* magazine's "The Fastest Female" feature of September 19, 1960, Wilma Rudolph was setting a feminine standard for white as well as black women: "From the moment she first sped down the track of Rome's Olympic Stadium, there was no doubt that she was the fastest woman the world had ever seen. But that was only part of the appeal of the shy, twenty-year-old Negro girl from Clarksville, Tenn. In a field of female endeavor in which the greatest stars have often been characterized by overdeveloped muscles and underdeveloped glands, Wilma ('Skeeter') Rudolph had long, lissome legs and a pert charm that caused an admiring Italian press to dub her 'the Black Pearl.' " (The documentary *Mr. Temple and the Tigerbelles* claims that the French called her "the Black Pearl," and the Italians "the Black Gazelle.") The Americans liked pacifying diminutives—at twenty she remained "a Negro girl" with a child's insect nickname.

Her long, lissome legs and pert charm should have carried the day for Denise and me. This was standard movie star soubrette praise that could have been used for Leslie Caron or Shirley MacLaine. Why were we so defensive?

Girls in our world and time had to struggle for permission to love sports, and their chances were better if they kept the love talk down. Sports weren't about to get them into good colleges. Sports weren't going to provide them with good professions after college. Sports weren't going to make them better marriage material. The serious pursuit of sports was for girls who didn't have other intellectual and social opportunities. We knew the drill. Girls like Denise and me were meant to prove that our people could do other things at least as well as we'd always done sports.

For the belittled, the depreciated and the despised, pride in an outstanding achievement stirs foreboding. (1) You fear a blunder will undermine it all: a flawed display of manners (a clumsy gesture, a speech pattern that's too rural, too black dialect-ical), which threatens to expose some aspect of the inferiority the achievement was supposed to disprove. (2) You dread public retaliation in some form: a renewed public insistence on your lacks; a reinvigorated belittling of your success.

Our own squeamishness was a self-administered, anticipatory punishment.

Denise and I were uneasily thrilled by the pace and stretch of the Tigerbelle limbs: muscle, sinew, bone pulsing along the track, torsos marching-band straight, shoulders evenly guiding the arms, up/down/back/forth;

bodies in white shorts trimmed with black and black tops trimmed in white. Bodies . . .

I started to write "bodies flagrant in . . ." or "bodies flaunting themselves in . . ." Those are the wrong words—not wrong to me at twelve in 1960, but wrong, so wrong, now. If the Tigerbelles had been white women, I'd have studied their bodies and uniforms with calm interest. I'd have noted the forthright competence of honed limbs and worked muscles. Not the rounded smoothness I craved at that stage of life, but not a threat. I would have been much less stirred by them, "stirred" meaning excited, invested and rattled.

The Tennessee Tigerbelles were the women's track team at historically black Tennessee State University. Their black coach, Mr. Ed Temple, groomed them for national and international success: "groomed" is the correct word, for they were taught, rehearsed, their diets, wardrobes, speech, grades tended to, via scrutiny, exhortation and reproof. They were servants for a greater cause and determined to prove they were the equal of male athletes. "If the boys can do it, you can!" said Mr. Ed Temple. His girl runners began winning Olympic medals in 1952, the same year that the historically white University of Tennessee admitted its first black student. (A man.)

—

I feared their publicity was inviting any and all white people to be on intimate terms with their bodies and their absolute will to win—to stretch, heave, grimace if need be as the finish line approached. Biological facts weren't facts. They were prompts. Prompts for race and sex presumptions. Denigrations.

Meanwhile, the Tigerbelles triumphed.

Olympic Medals

1952: A gold medal for precocious fifteen-year-old Barbara Jones.

1956: A bronze medal for the relay team.

1960: A gold medal for the relay team and two more gold medals for Wilma Rudolph, twenty—the first athlete of her sex to win that number.

In all, the club won twenty-three Olympic medals, thirty medals in the Pan American Games and thirty-four national team titles.

The fact is, I never worked as hard at anything, in high school or college, as Wilma Rudolph, Barbara Jones, Lucinda Williams and Martha Hudson worked to become Tennessee Tigerbelles.

Running to meet the best in themselves.

. . .

All of this comes rushing back to me as the International Olympic Committee enters the second decade of pondering and punishing the high testosterone levels of thirty-year-old black South African runner and gold medalist Caster Semenya. In 2009, the committee claimed she'd been taking drugs and so banned her from all women's competition. Further tests cleared her of drug charges but revealed what was called an "intersex trait" (high testosterone levels), which again was used to stop her from competing. In 2020 the committee ruled that *all* women athletes with higher than "normal" testosterone levels (it's called "a condition") must have them artificially reduced in order to compete with other female athletes. It used to be that "norms" were imposed through social myths and conventions; now they are enforced through biological ones. The will to prohibit stays unchanged. The power to oppose prohibition is recent and conditional. Semenya and others (most of them women of color) challenge these decisions and refuse to take hormones, supported by sports and human rights groups. They are still barred from certain races. And isn't hormone-reduction procedure a sanctioned form of drug abuse? A policy of biological pacification?

Semenya's is a victorious female body, from which *she has been severed by the Ruthless Hand of Wrong.*

Wilma, thou shouldst be living at this hour!

. . . .

Now I want to go back to these words: "Denise's legs were long, muscular and brown, like Wilma Rudolph's. But Denise was a dancer, and every week those forceful limbs of hers were being refined by ballet aesthetics."

Forceful, muscled brown limbs being refined by ballet. Denise gave herself to studying ballet. I studied it because I was supposed to. It was another way to be close to Denise's life. I paid close attention to Denise's passions. To her whims too. They were models I could imitate, adapt or make a point of rejecting. I watched how she handled prerogatives that would soon be mine: higher heels, longer manicured nails and brighter lipstick; boys who paid social calls at agreed-on hours; parties with lower lights and later curfews. Her will to argue with our parents—to proclaim her wishes—was impressive. And clamorous. I pondered her success and failure rates. The effort they took. I measured the cost of assertion or submission. She wanted to go to New York and dance. Our family admired that: as long, my parents made clear, as she finished college and (preferably) graduate school. Our parents went to New York to see Broadway shows and visit jazz clubs. Denise would go there to join the artists my parents could only watch. And dance was a way to belong with women whose art literally could not live without them.

Your girl's body was training its parts to acquire a language. And the work, so literal, so empirical, gave you special viewing rights in a world of theater and meticulous artifice: stage sets, costumes, pointe shoes, sumptuously plotted tales, charged moods and auras. You were dogged, faced with your limits in class (mine were FLAT FEET!). But in a theater (even watching film or TV) you were part of a vigilant, ecstatic corps.

Denise and I chose idols. Mine was Margot Fonteyn, all serene perfection. Denise claimed Maria Tallchief, all piercing angles and intensities. The names were flagrantly symbolic. *Margot,* protecting her eponymous worshipper; *Tallchief,* embodying leadership and non-white nobility. Whenever I hear ballet music from my youth—*The Nutcracker, Les Sylphides, Giselle, Coppélia, Firebird*—I relive my worship of these women. I worshipped their access to the exquisite and I worshipped how they labored for it. I want to emphasize how resolutely ballerinas worked to build and protect this fortress of exquisiteness.

I feel the racial imaginary creeping up on me, and my heart constricts. That zone of being not-white: its efficient exclusions, unacknowledged, reinforced, artfully disguised by the narrative of worship I've just written.

The enduring, exalted charisma of the ballet tradition, with its arduously evolved aesthetic.

Oh the expedient innocence of whiteness! It can call one thing—exclusion—by so many other names. Virtuous names like "tradition" and "aesthetic." And in fact (racial imaginary, advance no further!), if a non-white person has enough protections—money, cultural exposure, access to institutions that make exceptions ("we rarely accept Negroes as pupils, but in your daughter's case . . .")—she has access to the expedient innocence of privilege. And to those protected spaces in which the Jefferson daughters adore ballet, often with open hearts. An acting teacher friend of mine readies her students for auditions by telling them to imagine placing all the techniques and tools they've acquired into a barrel, and put it on like rodeo clowns do. Not to be glanced at or checked on anxiously, but to be with you and at the ready when the audition demands. Our psychic barrels contained race wariness, disappointment and a determination to play either defense or offense. Our expedient privilege allowed us to tuck those tools into our barrels until circumstances required their use.

V

What's in this critic's barrel of mine? Let's say I'm auditioning to play the part of a critic locked in conflict with a work of art that enchants and erases her. As so many ballets did. She must examine these contending forces in the art and in herself. She must pursue subtleties and ambiguities, study what's cruel or mean; enter states of exaltation and abjection.

Let me start by adapting Janet Malcolm's theatrically stern words about journalists. She writes: "Every journalist who is not too stupid or full of himself to notice what is going on knows that what he does is morally indefensible. He is a kind of confidence man, preying on people's vanity, ignorance, or loneliness, gaining their trust and betraying them without remorse."

I write:

Every critic who is not too stupid or full of herself to notice what is going on knows that what she does incites arrogance and hubris. She is a kind of omniscient narrator, preying on readers' vanity, insecurity and ambition, flattering their taste, sanctioning their beliefs, gaining their trust and betraying them without remorse.

Do you remember, readers, how excited I was earlier about that Jules Breton painting that gave Willa Cather's *The Song of the Lark* its title? Do you remember how my friend's chance remark about being competitive electrified me?

I'll call what follows: AN ACCOUNT OF MY LIFE WITH WILLA CATHER: INCIDENTS OF READING AND TEACHING HER DURING STRUGGLES OVER GENDER, RACE, CLASS AND ART IN THE PEDAGOGIC AND CRITICAL PRACTICES OF THE UNITED STATES. A TRUE STORY.

How I loved *The Song of the Lark*! How I loved Willa Cather's luminous portrait of a midwestern American girl becoming a great opera singer; a heroine shaping her destiny, not trapped by her fate. Call it the story of a girl who merges her inevitable growth into womanhood (encumbered word!) with a hard-won growth into art (exalted word!). Call it the taxonomy of a diva.

Can a taxonomy be luminous? Cather's is. That's her great gift, I think: to merge exacting observations with luminous perceptions. I started teaching women writers in the early nineties. When I thought about my own writing—its materials, its form, what needs would drive it—I wanted to learn from every one of them: from

Cather, Edith Wharton, Nella Larsen, Zora Neale Hurston, Elizabeth Bishop, Gwendolyn Brooks. I was also working out how to succeed as a teacher in the classroom, unprotected by a page and a byline.

I started teaching full-time in 2006. And I taught *The Song of the Lark* in college seminars between 2007 and 2011. *I loved it for the solace that it brought / And I loved her that she did offer it.* Many of you will recognize my source here—*Othello,* Act 1, Scene 3, where, grilled on what dark arts he hath used to win the fair Desdemona, the Moor replies: "She loved me for the dangers I had passed, / And I loved her that she did pity them. / This only is the witchcraft I have used."

Trusty Othello, always providing safe literary passage to the subject of race.

Nearly all of my students were young women; nearly all of them were young white women. And I realized after I'd taught *The Song of the Lark* a few times that I was uneasy; as I revised my notes, I knew I must find a sustained way to—which of these verbs is best?—expose, excavate, evaluate—the rapture stirred in Cather by her heroine's white skin. Less an insistent theme than a recurring motif of adjectives and similes. All the more treacherous, all the more seductive for that. Themes stir our consciousness; motifs pervade our unconscious. How, I asked myself, could I make potent the historical discord stirred by race worship without obliterating the novel's aesthetic concord?

It was a technical challenge, yes. I knew I had the necessary analytic tools, though: I'd been schooled in close reading; I'd kept up with African-American, post-colonial and feminist criticism. I was a book critic, for god's sake. I'd taught chapters of Toni Morrison's *Playing in the Dark: Whiteness and the Literary Imagination,* where Morrison examined Cather's last novel, *Sapphira and the Slave Girl.* It was set in Virginia, home of the Confederate ancestors Cather was sentimentally attached to all her life. But wasn't Morrison's task more straightforward than mine? She'd chosen a novel about slavery, a fumbling, uncertain (yet intriguing) novel, which she admired, rightly, much less than I admired *Lark.* She grappled with the novel's race gaps and struggles, its admissions and evasions, its lapses and ambivalences. She didn't have to grapple with her own. And she had the vast advantage of being Toni Morrison.

Here's my diagnosis of what really held me back. I knew that, if I revealed it too artlessly, my anger and grief at this white skin fetishism could overwhelm me and leave white students . . . what? Guilty but confused? Convinced but embarrassed? Dutiful but resentful? How not to endanger my authority as their professor, the black woman instructing them on our—and their—literary canon? How could I *initiate* them into rigorous distaste for the limits of Cather's racialized aesthetic, probe the sources of her racialized needs, map their repercussions? Teaching them to feel intellectual contempt was too easy. I wanted them to feel *chagrined*. Chagrin implicates those who feel it. And I wanted them to be *disappointed*—roundly disappointed in this major American writer Wilella Sibert Cather. As I'd had to be, time and time again, in a lifetime of reading white writers.

I remembered that in her drama critic days, Cather had found the art of concealment (practiced by Eleanora Duse) superior to that of disclosure (practiced by Sarah Bernhardt). To this end, I wondered: Were there registers of pity, even strategic empathy, I could use to expose this flaw of hers, this taint, this limitation in a work so expansively observed and imagined?

The pity I would teach my students must be clinical and unsparing. *Not* like Desdemona's pity for Othello, born of sympathy and erotic fascination. No, my pity would come from a close analysis of Cather's limits and vulnerabilities: of temperament and experience, of family and cultural history. I could pity Cather because for all her intelligence she could not free herself of these primal race needs and consolations. Rooted not just in history, but in her aesthetic and erotic core.

You can see that my pity had its vengeful core. How the proud, ardently self-made Cather would have loathed being its object! Aesthetics and eros—merging, diverging, wringing and twisting us every which way! Here my pity could even have an undertone of empathy. More emotional range would give me more power.

READER, THIS IS A PROCEDURAL. So I'll begin by recreating myself in teacher mode. Here I am, taking notes on the text. Expanding, supplementing what I said in 2010 or '11; making up for what I did not say then.

I.

The Song of the Lark is an epic, a lyric, and a Künstlerroman (novel of an artist's growth and education), filled, almost stuffed, with sensory, social and psychological detail; sweeping, at times bulky, rife with changing scenes, voices, moods and characters. And in all these ways it's true to opera, the form it honors. In it are modest towns, with their workaday routines (Thea's is Moonstone, Colorado). Brash cities, promoting art along with railroads and stockyards (Thea's is Chicago). The vast grandeur of western deserts (Thea's is Panther Canyon). The gilded glory of opera houses (Thea's is the Metropolitan). An America making itself up, using homemade rituals while seizing on (so as to absorb) great, inherited traditions: the art and architecture of the Sinagua people; the classical music and epic myth-building of Wagnerian opera. A portrait of the U.S. as a new world, clamorous yet slumberous, trying to make itself a coherent civilization.

I start my examination of the white rapture motif by cataloguing specific invocations of Thea's milky skin and flaxen locks: the basics any Nordic peasant would need to make herself a Wagnerian Rheingold goddess. Here are passages I marked in my copy of the 1988 Houghton Mifflin edition.

—As Moonstone's doctor, Dr. Howard Archie cares for a young, pneumonia-stricken Thea, lightly undressing her:

"As he lifted and undressed Thea he thought to himself what a beautiful thing a little girl's body was—like a flower. It was so neatly and delicately fashioned, so soft, so milky white." *If the eros of the passage makes you anxious, set your fears at rest. Dr. Archie is a good man and something of a eunuch. He recognizes Thea's gifts and does not presume to intrude on her body or psyche.*

—Fred Ottenburg, Thea's wealthy, worldly supporter, remarks:

"'The Jews always sense talent, and,' he added ironically, 'they admire certain qualities of feeling that are found only in the white races.'" I know that kind of irony—you mock your status while enhancing it. Self-congratulation and self-awareness holding the speaker upright between them.

—That influential patron, Mrs. Nathanmeyer, "a heavy, powerful old Jewess" with a "swarthy complexion" studying Thea:

"She caught the characteristic things at once: the free strong walk, the calm carriage of the head, the milky whiteness of the girl's arms and shoulders."

—Dr. Archie watches Thea, world-renowned at last:

". . . her attitudes, movements, her face, her white arms and fingers, everything was suffused with a rosy tenderness, a warm humility, a gracious and yet—to him—wholly estranging beauty."

A gracious and to him wholly estranging beauty. *Yes!* I'd found my objective correlative in Dr. Archie's alienation. He was alienated, intimidated by the great artist, who had usurped—devoured, consumed—the woman he once knew. It's what great artists do. They remove themselves from the circle of the normal and prosaic; they do it to us and for us. This transformation always thrills me. But now I was identifying with Howard Archie's estrangement. I was living it from my seat as a non-white spectator.

Through Thea, Cather envisions a formidable, seemingly comprehensive American classicism. And woefully, cursedly, that classicism needs the imprimatur of milky white skin.

This was the venom: whiteness as sign for the treasure America so covets, the treasure of great art. Europe its sacred fount.

A novelist uses every resource of her experience (what she's lived) and her imagination (what she wants to live). Both are forms of knowledge. For Cather both were impaired by Confederate Southern mythmaking: warrior angst; aristocrat elegy; belligerent disdain; wanton nostalgia. Negroes were former slaves with murky African origins: What did they have in common with the European immigrants bringing European ways and means to the Midwest she loved? Blacks weren't part of the usable past or aspirational future Cather was constructing for American art and culture.

Let me put it another way. They—we—American blacks—held no aesthetic appeal for her. She wasn't curious. She wasn't attracted—not intellectually, not sensually, not erotically. Blacks weren't part of the material she wanted for her world-building. What I wanted was for those choices to be evaluated and assessed as part of the longue-durée vision of American history and literature.

I still cherished memories of the early 1970s when the women's movement sent us blissfully hunting and gathering women writers. That's when I'd first read *Lark,* and cleaved unto Thea Kronborg. I had been utterly uninterested in Cather's novels before literary feminism spurred my curiosity and admiration. Now I honored this young midwestern woman, fierce and solitary, who sought the most valuable part of herself in something larger than herself. I longed for that. I nurtured, even coddled, my love for Cather's portrait of the artist as an obscure young woman. I cherished each personal connection (Chicago and the West, a people considered raw material for the making of a distinguished civilization). With care I noted that she admired the Mexican-Americans of Moonstone as the first "truly musical" people Thea meets; that she had no truck with the casual bigotry of certain local whites. I clung to Cather's luminous portrait of the "Ancient People," the Sinagua Indians of Arizona, whose art and architecture were America's classical heritage. I wanted my empathy to be unhindered by Cather's indifference, her dismissal of and disregard for any worthwhile role my people had played in the metamorphosis of American culture. And in those days my imaginative largesse had pleased me.

Now I felt I was being rebuffed and humiliated.

I let several years pass without speaking directly to Cather's whiteness rapture. The old stratagem, devised in childhood: not wanting to exclude myself from the cultural access whites had; not wanting to look damaged by what had been offered grudgingly or compensatorily. This no longer served. My inner life had to keep pace with the facts and furies of the outer world.

By revealing not just my anger, but my embarrassment, my wounded pride, my (dare I say) hurt, did I risk having white students turn their pity on me? Did I risk having my few non-white students cringe at my vulnerabilities? Don't all students want to challenge their teacher's authority and flaunt their own at least briefly? Once race pervaded our classroom, how easy for a white student to feel a certain satisfaction (call it relief, call it triumph) that she'd rarely (never?) had to put up with racial assaults on her self and soul? Could that give her license to pity—condescend to—me?

Re: my own pity practices. I'd worked hard to rid myself of rote condescension, especially around issues of class. But had I ever felt pity without some flicker of relief, signaling, "I'm so lucky to have been spared all that. I needn't brood and give way to futile resentments. I have the space to turn my thoughts elsewhere."

I didn't think my white students would do pity any better than I had. And I *did* brood on my racial grievances. I resented my students' leisure, their flowery beds of racial ease. I knew they all had their own sufferings, some of which *I'd* been spared—history doles out all kinds of suffering to all kinds of people. But their ancestors had made sure they were spared my kind of suffering. I brooded, I resented, I obsessed.

When I teach I like to display, even flaunt, the contours of my sensibility: teacher, thinker, reader, writer. The unspoken premise? Nothing I'd *chosen* to study and care for had lethally damaged me, whatever its racial intent. (Conscious, careless, mocking, vicious.) The power to imagine what couldn't or wouldn't imagine me was my protection. My magic helmet, my anthem and aria. I could be wounded, I could suffer, I could rage, but these weapons shielded me from permanent harm. When I attacked the bigotries of race or of gender, I attacked calmly. With pointed historical evidence. With logic. With irony.

No scars marked the smooth skin of my thoughts. No keloids.

My white students were not to be allowed to indulge—"to entertain"—the notion that they were luckier than I. They were to admire my well-made weapons. And not just admire: they were to envy them and long for them.

2.

To further my Cather inquiries, I was reading Cather's criticism: the confident reviews she'd published as a young journalist when fiction was the mighty sword she had yet to claim. She had charm as well as authority. But she wasted no charm on what she considered second-rate or smugly minor. And she made clear that her standards brooked no sentimental lapses, none of the emotional hyperbole she condemned in women writers like Kate Chopin. She wanted her place in the select portrait gallery of high-minded, high-handed male critics and artists.

Eventually, I came upon her short 1894 review of Blind Tom Wiggins, the black piano prodigy who toured the country (more accurately, was toured by white promoters) for more than fifty years. Wiggins was a former slave with prodigious musical gifts, a pianist-composer who, apart from being blind, suffered from tremors and speech disorders (now diagnosed as Asperger's or autism). Cather was intrigued and repelled. Tom spoke of himself and "his own idiocy" in the third person, she wrote;

he applauded himself. He was a living phonograph, "a sort of animated memory with sound-producing powers." Her tone combined anthropological distance with *noli me tangere* distaste.

"There was an insanity, a grotesque horribleness about it that was interestingly unpleasant," she continued. (Interestingly unpleasant: a flicker of the adolescent Cather so immersed in medical science.)

The fact of his talent all but offends her: "It was as if the soul of a Beethoven had slipped into the body of an idiot." His gifts—"He played with genius"—only arouse her need to belittle him—"for certainly that may be called genius which has no basis in intellect."

And then comes an unexpected admission, like a dissonance that refuses to resolve. "One laughs at the man's queer antics, and yet, after all, the sight is not laughable. It brings us too near the things we sane people do not like to think of."

Those last words hint at the layered awareness one is used to valuing in Cather. *"Too near the things we sane people do not like to think of"* (italics mine). "We" do not like to think of bodies marked by uncontrollable shaking, eyes gone blind; a slave child at his mistress's piano, so terrified when he hears her voice that he plunges into fits and fevers that last for days; bodies that disgust even as they produce art that enchants us.

REMEMBER: THIS IS A PROCEDURAL. WE'RE INVESTIGATING A CULTURAL SITE SOME OF WHOSE MATERIALS HAVE BEEN IGNORED OR MISIDENTIFIED.

A character based on Tom Wiggins called Blind D'Arnault appears in *My Ántonia,* a novel published three years after *Lark.* And I know perfectly well . . . wait, let me start again: "perfectly well" is too defensive . . . And I know that the way D'Arnault is described—the tone, the words, the benign condescension—is in character for the novel's narrator, Jim Burden.

Jim has come west after a boyhood in Virginia. He is reasonably observant, reasonably thoughtful and, when the romantic in him is stirred, emotionally responsive. He is never deeply imaginative, as Cather makes clear on every page of the novel. So of course, when he encounters Blind D'Arnault, he'll mingle antebellum race nostalgia with music appreciation.

Cather often uses ethnic generalities (physical and temperamental) with affection and respect. These generalities are comfort tropes, usually countered by precise descriptions and characterizations. Here they work as crude Darwinian confines.

"He had the Negro head . . . almost no head at all . . . ," Jim says of D'Arnault, and instead of close-cropped hair he has "close-cropped wool." (Cather has softened his appearance by making him a mulatto.) As for the tremors and the compulsive repeating of words and sounds: "He would have been repulsive if his face had not been so kindly and happy." A Negro's kindly happiness is the only possible antidote to his behavioral and biological repulsiveness.

When Jim describes the child D'Arnault first hearing the piano, Cather gives him eloquent, sensuous language. "Through the dark he found his way to the Thing, to its mouth. He touched it softly and it answered softly, kindly. He shivered and stood still."

Lovely. A deep and dazzling darkness. A spiritual awakening.

Then Jim returns to the comforts of condescension. D'Arnault's white Southern teachers found he had perfect pitch and an exceptional memory, he explains, but D'Arnault wore them out; he couldn't learn like other people; couldn't acquire finish. ("Other people" being sighted people, people untouched by autism, people unbound by slavery.) "He was always a Negro prodigy who played barbarously and wonderfully." ("Negro" and "barbarously" imposing firm constraints onto "prodigy" and "wonderfully.") "As piano playing it was perhaps abominable," Jim muses, "but as music it was something real, vitalized by a sense of rhythm that was stronger than his other physical senses—that not only filled his dark mind, but worried his body incessantly." To watch and listen as D'Arnault played plantation melodies for the happy Nebraskans "was to see a Negro enjoying himself as only a Negro can."

What a banal conclusion! We're talking about a major writer here—of course she could have given some dissonant texture to Jim's observations. She's constructed his character with limits from start to finish. He misses plenty about the Ántonia he worships, about her reality as opposed to his vision of her. With Ántonia, Cather knows and shows what Jim misses. With D'Arnault, she can't.

STOP! Collect yourself, Professor Jefferson. You've spent all this time on a scene that's not even in *The Song of the Lark.*

But I'm supplying context and subtext. I'm mapping some of the neural pathways by which a vision of culture develops. I'm going to try a version of those blind symphony orchestra auditions where the minority candidate plays from behind a screen to guard against the usual race and gender biases. Let's pretend I'm speaking from behind a screen, to students who have never seen me.

Serious readers do their research, I say. They question, they pursue, they collect and weigh evidence; they consider informed speculations. They study the relations between an artist's criticism and their fiction.

3.

Thea has left Moonstone, Colorado, to study music in Chicago. One afternoon she goes to a concert and hears Dvořák's *New World* Symphony for the first time.

Dvořák had written ardently about "Negro spirituals" as a foundation for American music; also about the grand and spacious plains of the Midwest. Cather would have known this. Thea wouldn't have: she was still a young, provincial student. So when the first movement ends and the Largo theme begins, all she sees and feels is her own western home—"the sand hills, the grasshoppers and locusts, all the things that wakened and chirped in the early morning; the reaching and reaching of high plains, the immeasurable yearning of all flat lands." Lyric. Sensuous. Melodic.

I wanted my students to know that when Cather the critic reviewed the Pittsburgh Orchestra's performance of Dvořák's *New World* Symphony in 1897, she began by reminding her readers that it was built around "the old Negro airs of the South." Strange, she wrote, that the only folk music we have was given to us by "our slaves."

She'd thought there was little there beyond "Dixie" and "Swing Low, Sweet Chariot" until, on a recent trip to Virginia, she heard Negroes singing, "their wordless minor melodies echoing through the silver silence of the Virginia moonlight." With a brief homage to Stephen Foster, she heads North as fast as she can, declaring that after the symphony's first movement, Dvořák has "pretty well exhausted his African theme." (How did it suddenly become an alien African theme rather than a national American one?) The South fades away, the limitless Midwest emerges; one can hear the confident, almost ecstatic swell of Cather's voice, so relieved at coming home to "limitless prairies" filled with the "peasantry of all the nations of Europe," who offer the world their collective "song of a homesick heart."

I must be clear. I did not need Cather to supply a brief passage in which Thea's wise music teacher tells her about the influence of spirituals on this symphony, in particular about the black singer, arranger and composer Harry Burleigh. It was Burleigh, Dvořák's student assistant at New York's National Conservatory of Music, who introduced him to spirituals. And it was Burleigh's arrangements of spirituals that broke new ground for soloists in classical music. Until Burleigh published *Jubilee Songs of the United States of America* in 1916, writes musicologist Eileen Southern, "spirituals were performed only in ensemble or choral arrangements on the concert stage." So yes, I'd have mightily enjoyed such a passage. But I didn't need it.

Or so I thought. My compensation is that music history has long since proved Cather wrong. *New Yorker* critic Alex Ross sums it up well in a 2010 essay on Dvořák, writing crisply, "In the English-horn solo in the Largo of the 'New World' he created an ersatz spiritual, which was later given lyrics and a title, 'Goin' Home.' "

We critics leave our factual errors behind for all to see—our errors, our evasions, our simplifications and dismissals: what we didn't know or didn't care to know about the art we loved.

And how cleanly, relentlessly, Cather (as critic and novelist) excises the "African theme" from Dvořák. Like a surgeon amputating a limb. Except the limb's not all gone in the novel. It leaves its trace on the final description of what Thea hears in the Largo: "There was home in it too, the amazement of a new soul in a new world; a soul new and yet old, that had dreamed something despairing, something glorious in the dark before it was born; a soul obsessed by what it did not know, under the cloud of a past it could not recall." These words could almost be read as an evocation of those Negro American sorrow songs, which did indeed shape Dvořák's "ersatz spiritual." But they remain coded, unconscious. And possibly my own invention.

Cather couldn't or wouldn't imagine that music came to Blind Tom Wiggins in a lucid sensuous form, just as it came to Thea in the Sinagua ruins of Arizona. "And now her power to think seemed converted into a power of sustained sensation. She could become a mere receptacle . . . or become a color . . . or she could become a continuous repetition of sound . . ." And that I hold against her.

4.

Willa Cather, I know your Virginia mother, former belle and beauty, holding fast to the ancestral memory of her privilege as she held fast to her riding crop and whip—we know not which slaves or servants she applied them to, but we know she applied them to the bodies of her children. We know she was disappointed with the physical attributes of her stocky, brainy daughter, with dark hair and features that lacked ingratiating curves. A daughter impatient with adults who tried to cuddle her, who at age nine jumped back from an avuncular family friend, a good old Virginia judge, with the words "I'se a dangerous nigger I is!" By age fourteen the "dangerous nigger" had become the daring Will (or William) Cather, M.D., who got himself a boy's haircut, strode through town in a man's suit and cap, and dissected animals to prepare for his career in surgery. Then to university, to arts criticism and magazine journalism. And through it all, the struggling aspiring novelist; the woman who fell in love with women she could not win, then brought her fascination with them to the page, making herself into the manly narrators who draw their portraits and mourn their troubled fates.

Willa Cather, I know something about your abjection, your compensatory drives, your erotic and emotional needs; how you made yourself into a vessel that could contain longing and rapture; desire never assuaged but never renounced.

The women you first loved: those white arms, that wide throat, the beauty that, like the Lorelei's, threatened to destroy you because you wanted so to possess it, merge with it.

You could not. Weren't you as removed from that lyrical whiteness as I am? Because you were plain. Didn't you risk being excluded from certain kinds of privilege and acceptance? Because you were a lesbian.

Surely all this drove you to imagine and interpret what had not imagined you.

I've had to do the same.

. . .

AN ENTR'ACTE

This confessing and reckoning have exhausted me. I need an imaginative break. I need to restore myself. Stage encounters with black artists who knew how talented and complicated they were, and who insisted that the world know it too. I need speculation instead of argument.

Last year when I was getting ready to teach several Baldwin essays, I sent away for the December 1966 issue of *Playboy* so I could read a long interview with him. That same issue turned out to have an interview with Sammy Davis, Jr.

And suddenly they came together in my mind, like two stars making a one-night-only joint appearance. Baldwin using his voice and body to represent the collective black experience; Davis absorbing that collective experience into his singular voice and body.

They are born one year apart: Jimmy in 1924, Sammy in 1925. To be a chosen messenger for your people, it seems one must begin as a gifted child chosen by adults.

You are Sammy Davis, Jr., and you have been a song and dance virtuoso in theaters, clubs and films since you were three years old.

You are James Baldwin and you have been writing

since you were in elementary school. Having a play performed by your class when you're nine and a half isn't the same as being the title character in a twenty-minute film titled *Rufus Jones for President* when you're eight. (Sammy did that.) But you keep writing plays and songs and one of them wins you a congratulatory letter from Mayor La Guardia. By the age of fourteen you are a Harlem evangelist with a pulpit and an audience of enthralled parishioners.

"Whose little boy are you?" Bishop Rosa Artemis Horn asked you, little Baldwin, when you were preparing to be saved. *Why yours of course,* you answered. "Yours" would come to mean Everyone's. Everyone with eyes to see and ears to hear.

The white American world demanded an uncanny black man—uncannily gifted, and uncannily willing to shoulder, wrap himself in, become one with the needs and desires of American whites and blacks.

The forbidden hung over you both in secret. You, Baldwin, were a homosexual; you, Davis, a heterosexual who attracted and pursued white women. You were both skinny and short: Jimmy 5'6", Sammy 5'5". You were odd-looking. Jimmy, you had pop eyes and a nose still considered Negro-broad; Sammy, you had a wide forehead that sloped into a long nose, which drew attention downward to a slightly protruding lower lip. (After that

1954 car crash, you had a glass eye too.) This gave those who still craved it a last chance to see your gifts as compensation for what you so obviously lacked: the superiority of the Normal.

Let Baldwin use "We" again and again to implode the cognitive certainties of race. Let Davis declare that every time he walks out on a stage he's swaggering through the saloon door of a rough and rowdy town to prove he's the fastest gun in the West.

Both with a portmanteau of dictions and accents: Anglo–New York theater; Jewish and Black vaudeville; queer dandy; hetero swinger; lofty evangelist; breezy nightclub MC. All to conquer, persuade, uplift, titillate, intimidate, exhilarate: to prove their value to the world. To prove our value to the world.

BALDWIN: I'm bound to question an ethic or a way of life or a system of reality which has nearly destroyed me and which obviously intends to destroy my children . . . One begins to feel despairing, one begins to feel foolish; and one begins to dig beneath the bequeathed realities in the hope of arriving at a new coherence and a new strength, in the hope, in fact, of being released from an incipient schizophrenia. But at that moment, the moment one begins to pull away in order to see, one is accused of thinking "black." But I don't really know what thinking "black" means—except that it seems to pose a threat to people who think, I suppose, "white."

DAVIS: I always go onstage anticipating what people out there may be feeling against me emotionally, I want to rob them of what they're sitting there thinking:

Negro. With all the accompanying clichés. Ever since I recognized what prejudice is, I've tried to fight it away, and the only weapon I could use was my talent. Away back, when I was learning the business, I had no education, no power, no influence; entertaining was the only way I had to change prejudiced thinking.

They learned early in life: If you can't be free, be a prodigy.

. . .

Think of what now follows as an experiment in Anglo-, Afro- and Retro-futurism. Appropriation. Miscegenation. Illicit collaborations.

The Lifted Veil, by George Eliot. *The Souls of Black Folk,* by W. E. B. Du Bois. Which one was I reading when I suddenly thought of the other? I put the first book down, I pulled the second from my shelf, and started comparing them, line by line.

George Eliot had dark hair, pale skin, a long face and full lower lip, a prominent nose that widened slightly at the nostrils and that some portraits give a suggestion of a hook to. She could, in fact or fancy, be read as Jewish or as some mixed-race combination of black, white and indigenous.

W. E. B. Du Bois had tawny brown skin and crinkly hair: he was a black man of mixed descent (African, English, Dutch and Huguenot). The small, even features, the narrow nose (often called patrician), the Van Dyke beard give him a physiognomy that could easily be read as white.

ELIOT: Are you unable to imagine this double consciousness at work within me, flowing on like two parallel streams which never mingle their waters and blend into a common hue?

DU BOIS: One ever feels his two-ness—an American, a Negro; two souls, two thoughts, two unreconciled strivings; two warring ideals in one dark body whose dogged strength alone keeps it from being torn asunder.

See them in this common world! Watch, listen as they explore the torment of double consciousness across two races, two nations, two genders and two generations.

George Eliot publishes *The Lifted Veil* in 1859. W. E. B. Du Bois publishes *The Souls of Black Folk* in 1903.

She invents the voice of an English gentleman; he creates the voice of an American Negro gentleman-scholar. For both, the veil is the torment of "double consciousness" in a harsh and unjust society; the burden of second sight, whereby one perceives

"all the suppressed egoism, all the struggling chaos of puerilities, meanness . . . and indolent make-shift thoughts of others . . ." (Eliot)

and endures seeing oneself through their eyes,

"measuring one's soul by the tape of a world that looks on in amused pity and contempt." (Du Bois)

Du Bois wrote his own gothic fictions and his own proto-Victorian novel. Did he read *The Lifted Veil*? If so, it appears nowhere in his carefully kept reading list.

In the many chronicles of his intellectual life, sources for his use of double consciousness include Hegel, Lamarck, William James, Emerson and Goethe. I choose the possibility of this furtive, illicit connection between him and Eliot. Brilliant and driven, both of them. Grandly ethical. Achieving fame and honor, yet denied so much because of gender and race.

Eliot had never used a male narrator before *The Lifted Veil* and she never would again; neither would she venture into the lurid regions of gothic and science fiction. *Daniel Deronda,* her novel exploring the racialized bigotry of anti-Semitism, was twenty years off. It's as if she was reaching into the future with this tale, summoned there to intuit forthcoming cultural narratives.

Du Bois, like Eliot, is a driven writer and scholar. He's crafting a persona for his analytic, speculative and autobiographical book. So perhaps he takes up, appropriates the evocative Veil metaphor? Perhaps it's unconscious. Then he deepens and expands the portrait of a cultivated man, belittled by conventional society, forced into psychic solitude, preternaturally attuned to the world's cruelties. He joins that individual soul to a collective one engaged in historical struggles.

ELIOT: I began to be aware of a phase in my abnormal sensibility . . .

DU BOIS: I remember well when the shadow swept across me.

ELIOT: This was the obtrusion on my mind of the mental process going forward in first one person, and then another . . .

DU BOIS: I was different from the others or like mayhap in heart and life and longing, but shut out from their world by a vast veil . . .

ELIOT: I might have believed this importunate insight to be merely a diseased activity of the imagination but that my prevision of incalculable words and actions proved it to have a fixed relation to the mental processes in other minds.

DU BOIS: The Negro is a sort of seventh son, born with a veil and gifted with second sight in this American world . . . a world which yields him no self-consciousness but only lets him see himself through the revelation of the other world . . .

ELIOT: . . . this superadded consciousness, wearying and annoying enough when it urged on me the trivial experience of indifferent people, became an intense pain and grief when it seemed to be opening to me the souls of those who were in a close relation to me—their characters, were seen and thrust asunder by a microscopic vision that showed all the intermediate frivolities, all the suppressed egoism, all the struggling chaos of puerilities, meanness, vague capricious memories, and indolent make-shift thoughts . . .

DU BOIS: It is a peculiar sensation, this double-consciousness, this sense of always looking at one's self through the eyes of others, of measuring one's soul by the tape of a world that looks on in amused pity and contempt.

When *The Lifted Veil* ends, Eliot's dying narrator is alone and in despair, still trapped in a consciousness *from which human words and deeds emerge like leaflets covering a fermenting heap.*

When *The Souls of Black Folk* ends, Du Bois is exhorting the world to **"Rend the veil."**

Hear my cry, O God the Reader; vouchsafe that this my book fall not still-born into the world wilderness. Let there spring from out its leaves vigor of thought and thoughtful deed . . . may infinite reason turn the tangle straight, and these crooked marks on a fragile leaf be not indeed

THE END

How hard they worked to be the visionaries the future needed. They would have made a handsome couple, could he have borne a woman of equal talents and she a man of alien caste and hue. I think they've earned a respite. So let's join them together now, give them a stately turn in that idyllic cultural space Du Bois imagined beyond the color line, "where smiling men and women glide in gilded halls."

VI

For a time, he and I made a striking couple. We always began our Manhattan nights in pseudo-gilded restaurants. We were spared the more extreme constraints of race and gender. And we were a striking couple that winter of 1997. My father had died just before Christmas: "my system's shutting down," he'd say in those last months as he took or hid his daily ration of pills; as he faced his memory lapses. "This mind used to hold so much," he told my mother the day he had to ask if he'd remembered their phone number correctly.

What luck, a few months after his death, to be galvanized by lust!

And for a good six years I found my Afro-Brazilian lover acutely desirable. He had the dark skin and meticulously carved features I'd fetishized in my youth. He had the aura of sexual ruthlessness that myth bestows on this type. He wasn't a buck in the least, though; he was a buccaneer. (Buccaneers are allowed to have brains; bucks aren't.)

There was a type of gentleman gangster who figured alluringly in twentieth-century black life. He didn't litter the neighborhood with drugs, he ran the numbers, which could be thought of as a form of entertainment; he never boasted of strong-arming rivals, though he must have. He dressed in well-cut suits. Sometimes he had respectably bourgeois parents, a college degree and good, if slightly flashy, manners. He was a lowlife high achiever.

My Afro-Brazilian lover was a high achiever in a highly reputable profession.

"You're very different from the women he usually has affairs with," a friend reported. She meant they were usually natural blondes, whose skin ranged from cream to alabaster with a touch of pink. I pretended not to be flattered. When I couldn't ignore a persistent twinge of satisfaction, I practiced being wry.

He was sexually passionate and emotionally chilly. I never stopped being flattered by his attention. I moved between circumstantial abjection (waiting for his calls and his visits) and an onsite hauteur that I tried to keep from being shrill. It was relentless and it was often thrilling. And gradually, by degrees, it began to pall. He was involved with others; I was not. That made our ongoing wants incompatible. That made my continuous want demeaning.

Five years in, I went to a friend's play reading. "Everything changes when you have no hope," the lead character said about her dwindling love affair. I made her words mine. I began to recite them to myself. Regularly. Forcefully. Nothing would change, I repeated: not around us, not between us, not inside us.

Some months later I proposed an end. We were in a restaurant, and we'd finished our dinner. He concurred. We finished our wine. Our words were brief; our manners contained. He was taken aback, I could sense it. But he admitted nothing. We parted with practiced calm.

I brooded, though. I grieved, I wanted to imagine endings that had more texture.

FIRST ENDING

When I grieve my mind becomes a public domain for rhymes, fragments, phrases, bits of song. They surge into my ears and throat. They patter and intone until I arrange them to my own ends.

When lovely woman stoops to folly and
Paces about her room again, alone . . .

I wasn't going to be patronized by T. S. Eliot. I hadn't stooped to folly. I'd chosen to partner it.

Oh the blues ain't nothing but a slow-aching heart disease
Just like consumption killing me by degrees.

I felt I could work with this Ida Cox lyric. I'd get rid of her continuous present and put "killing" in the safely dead past tense. *"Just like consumption, it killed me by degrees."*

Yet here I was. Undead and alert. I needed a way to ease myself into the past perfect tense, where the flesh can hold memory and possibility. Why not a touch of Virginia Woolf?

Yes, I said, laying down my grief in acute delight, I have had my vision.

SECOND ENDING

Here I think of our parting as a restaging of the last scene between Snoop and Mike in *The Wire*. They're in a car together at night. Mike pulls a gun on Snoop, sensing she's about to do the same to him. Snoop turns, takes a sangfroid glance at her image in the car window and runs a casual hand across her head. *How my hair look, Mike?* she asks. Honoring her sangfroid, he answers: *You look good girl,* then shoots her in the head. In my version we shoot each other, exit, through opposite doors, and walk off in opposite directions.

No backward glances. Nothing but flesh wounds.

. . .

At this point I could take to my bed again, keep up the brooding and grieving. I'll exercise instead, have my hair colored and cut. Reorganize my energies and my focus. Dip into history and literature with an expanded cast of women performers and commentators.

I'm rereading *Measure for Measure,* I tell a friend. I don't like it, he says. Those overplotted shenanigans.

I like it, I tell him. I like intelligent virgins. Shakespeare had to go into overdrive to find a plot that would make fiercely chaste Isabella comply with patriarchy's demands.

I've liked—loved—intelligent virgins since I was a child, starting with Daphne, the god-pursued nymph, and Cassandra, the unheeded prophet. Gifted, willful. Beauties too. And punished for it all. One turned into a tree; one turned into a slave, then a concubine, then a corpse.

In *Measure for Measure,* until the plot traps her, Isabella's virginity is the source of her unimpeded will.

In nineteenth-century Massachusetts, Emily Dickinson's virginity was a source of unimpeded vision.

Marianne Moore gave it a modernist's transgressive brio: marriage, like Victorian diction, was an enterprise "requiring all one's criminal ingenuity to avoid"!

The Criminal Virgin plots her way to a practice unimpeded by the regulatory laws of the patriarchs.

But the word ***virginity*** is too shrouded in punitive hierarchies. ***Chastity*** is more generous, more generative.

Chastity is the will and wish to shape one's life apart from unsought patriarchal interventions. One's literal sexuality isn't the issue. Chastity can be erotic, or reposeful. It can be an imaginative abyss deep enough to plunge into with gusto.

Marianne Moore

"What of chastity? It confers a particular strength," she said.

The year was 1972 and day after day I sat on a sofa bed in my studio apartment reading women writers feverishly. How brave, I thought, how brave.

This virgin
Unimpeded, unashamed,
"Lit by piercing glances from within."

"Thank you for showing me your father's autograph," she said, and returned to her own concerns.

I do these
things which I do, which please
No one but myself.

Valiantly curious, discreetly voracious,

Acknowledging the social and spiritual forces which had made her.

Never never will I marry,
Never never will I wed.
Born to wander solitary,
Wide my world, narrow my bed.

Moore, born to wander solitary, wide her world of plants, animals, museum objects, artifacts, historical ethical matters.

What of "chastity" when one shares a daily life, a single bed, and a literary language with one's mother?

Harriet Jacobs (REDUX)

She said: "Reader, my story ends with freedom; not in the usual way with marriage." Life and literature have generally failed to invest in Negro virgins unless they're precocious children or imperiled adolescents. Was this an aspiration of mine? But as a girl I was longingly, intensely romantic, eager to claim the destiny of, say, the fiercely chaste and beautiful Atalanta, ultimately outrun and claimed by a Lover.

So here and now the point is: to claim or reclaim, strategically, longingly, for concentration or relaxation, not the sanctity of virginity, but the solace of chastity.

Think of the adolescent slave Harriet Jacobs, aching to maintain her chastity as a form of selfhood: strategizing to resist the sexual threats of a vicious and repulsive master; claiming the privilege of "choosing" a lover, a slaveholder too but a comely one, with manners that gave her the illusion of being courted, which is the illusion of choosing; bearing two children—no choice there—and then plotting her own disappearance and escape by hiding in her grandmother's attic for seven years, till she could flee North, secure freedom for her children and re-form herself in life and literature as a chaste heroine and mother.

Requiring All One's Criminal Ingenuity to Avoid: For Marianne Moore, this was Marriage.

Requiring All One's Criminal Ingenuity to Achieve:
For Harriet Jacobs this was Chastity.
The Body at peace.
Alone with itself at last.

. . .

Women's anger needs to be honored—celebrated and protected—the way virginity used to be! Female anger is a discipline, a repertory of styles. Each requires vocal, gestural, emotional skills; a clear sense of what the situation offers and how the story unfolds. Growing girls need anger models. Muses. Coaches and exemplars. What works best? Tempestuous fury; amused disdain; quiet (but not temperate) resistance?

The child is not mother to the woman as in Wordsworth's stately formulation. She's a disruptive part who gets quashed, reduced to a heap of remnants **["remnant": noun: . . . chips, cuttings, fragments, or other small pieces of raw material removed, cut away, flaked off, etc., in the process of making or manufacturing an item]**.

The Middle School Years (late 1950s)

Sixth grade: When I was done with Beth, my sweetly dead Alcottian Little Woman, I wanted transitional figures—adults who could still evoke innocence, along with erotic stirrings. Deborah Kerr's refined heart palpitations; the purified sensuality of Jean Simmons. Diahann Carroll: dreamy ingénue and buoyant soubrette.

Sustained displays of anger haven't claimed my attention yet. Being the center of attention has.

***Seventh and eighth grade* (1959–60, pushed into one arduous "Pre-Freshman" year at my school):**

I realized I needed daredevils.

Dorothy Parker proves a girl could be a gun moll, whether she's on the town or at her desk.

"What can you say when a man asks you to dance with him?

"I most certainly will not dance with you. I'll see you in hell first. Why thank you, I'd love to but I'm having labor pains . . ."

Assignment: memorize her dead-end noir poems. Literary girls can flaunt existential dread. "Resumé": Recite her snappy catalogue of suicide options with gusto. "Coda": Indulge in a shiver of recognition at the lines "This living, this living, this living / Was never a project of mine." In our school's Voice Speaking Choir performance that spring, a guy—an intellectual senior—recites Parker's "Coda," twisting his limbs into a ball to mock-keen the closing lines: "So I'm thinking of throwing the battle / Would you kindly direct me to hell?" It's on the same program as "The Hollow Men": Mrs. Parker's keeping company with Mr. Eliot.

Literary boys can run, but they can't hide.

I see *West Side Story* onstage. I play "America" over and over on the record player. Toss my head, arch my back, try to imitate the curl and lash of Chita Rivera's Puerto Rican accent. I kick and sashay as best I can. Chita is cheeky, sexy, clever. And Latins are a deluxe signifier for

Negroes on stage and screen, an alluring, enviable edition of non-white people with histories not wholly bound to the history of slavery in the United States.

I work to develop anger chops. Stride through the house as Mama Rose in *Gypsy.* Start with the climax of "Some People," this stage mother's manifesto of grit and vision. As for the humdrum folk who've "got the dream [yeah] but not the guts": Mount the stairs as the orchestra mounts for Ethel Merman's final boast: "Well, they can stay and rot . . . [every note's a clean uppercut] But not-Ro-OSE"!!!!!!!! Hands flung out, head flung back. I then make my way through the whole record, readying myself for that final soliloquy where, center stage, Rose excoriates her daughters and wills herself to rise in triumph from the ashcan of her life.

"Everything's coming up Roses this time for Me! FOR ME! FOR ME!" (grab on to that last ME and hold tight).

FEBRUARY 1959. Behold Nina Simone's debut album cover, *Little Girl Blue*. She sits on a bench in Central Park legs curled up, head in hand. Musing, brooding—the way girls and young women do when they're alone. (There are so many portraits of girls and women reading. Why not more of girls and women alone with their bodies, thinking and dreaming? That's the quality of her music.)

Nina Simone is twenty-six. She wears black pants and

a big red-and-black buffalo plaid jacket. Well-cut lace-up walking shoes. Unabashed red lipstick on unabashed full lips. Skin a "deep killer brown." (I quote Bessie Smith's phrase to offer posthumous dash.) And as I wrote those last two sentences, Simone's face reminded me of Michaela Coel's in her 2015–17 TV series, *Chewing Gum;* sixty years on, it still caused fits of viewer consternation. Big red lips on dark skin: a physiognomy and cosmetic malfunction. (SHE HAS ONLY HERSELF TO BLAME jeered the makeup vixen who still crouches in the mirrors and minds of women.)

In 1959, would I have preferred Miss Simone to be a lighter brown? Yes.

Nevertheless, my friends and I are besotted with Nina Simone. Our parents buy her album. Some of us buy our own copies, listen alone in our rooms, then talk about it together; marvel at the non-womanly—by which we meant non-soprano, non-limpid voice she brings to "I Loves You, Porgy." She isn't in thrall to Bess's warring desires; they're in thrall to what she chooses to make of them.

She will make them into a monologue, thoughtful but driven. It could even be a soliloquy, as if Bess were working through, preparing what she knows she must tell Porgy; summoning a dream of domestic peace, reliving scenes of lust and surrender.

JAZZ AS PLAYED IN AN EXCLUSIVE SIDE STREET CLUB, the album cover promises: when this young woman leaves her Central Park bench in this photo she will lead us to a suave sanctum of low lights and intimate tables with bodies close together; the sound of cocktail glasses, of murmuring voices, then rapt silence, and eager, discreet applause.

Simone sings love songs. Love squandered, love neglected, love withdrawn or never really offered. And she complicates these songs. "Little Girl Blue" mourns her lost self as much as any lost man. She makes that pliant lament, "Mood Indigo," pound and brood. "Love Me or Leave Me" usually flaunts its desperation; Simone uses bop blues and Bach counterpoint to make it a form of self-examination.

High School: The sixties commence. Bringing heels, not flats, Tampax, not Kotex, straight skirts that highlight what pleated skirts mute: your butt and your thighs.

CUTE is everywhere. Saucy, winsome cute (Diana Ross and the Supremes); perky, carbonated cute (Sandra Dee as *Gidget*); jaunty, sensible cute (Doris Day and Mary Tyler Moore); offbeat gamine cute (Shirley MacLaine and Audrey Hepburn).

Find exemplars in your own race. Play your 45s attentively. The rasped defiance of Mary Wells framing the words "Bye Bye Baby" with two cute-eviscerating gospel "WHOOOOOOOOO!"s. Follow Etta James's pivot from the torch tendresse of "At Last" to the fists-up taunt of "Pushover." Tempting lips, wavy hair, pretty eyes, come-hither stare, she lists and discards each one.

"You took me for a Puh-uh-uh-USH-over" is the refrain. "Whoa, you thought I was a"—and here she catches "PUSH" in a wrestler's hold and throws it down over and over, pinning it to the mat. It lies there panting feebly, then expires. Etta leaves the ring, eyebrow pencil unsmudged, cat's eyeliner unsmeared, fluffy blonde coif intact. The six strands of her crystal earrings vibrate slightly as she walks.

In the early '60s we fritter about; here a defiant glance, there a resolute lift of the chin. Trying to avoid the bright moments, bad-end scenarios. The ones where the reckless girl is disgraced, the scheming woman eliminated.

Denise has a high art conversion experience with Martha Graham in 1962, when she studies at Connecticut College's summer dance program. It's Medea she's smitten by, Medea pulling the red ribbon of bile and vengeance out of her stomach. Denise raves. Denise demonstrates the Graham contraction: the muscles of the pelvis and abdomen pull inward, as if the dancer was a sculptor carving her own torso out of space. Graham and her dancers (including brown-skinned Matt Turney, including brown-skinned Mary Hinkson): contracting, crouching, elevating, spiraling. Denise could use Turney and Hinkson as models of what was possible (it was possible—yes!—to be a major Negro dancer in a major white dance company), but she couldn't let herself worship them as she worshipped Graham. Turney was too reserved in manner, too lyrical. A sacrifice (Cassandra) rather than an avenger (Clytemnestra). An American Pioneer Woman, not a legendary heretic or sorceress.

Mary Hinkson did have ferocity. But our mother called her Bunny; they'd been sorority sisters. The shadow of Good Home Training clung to her offstage, which was the last thing Denise wanted—likewise the shadow of parental demands that one be the perfect offspring, not the questing original.

Graham will accompany Denise through her adult life, as will Bette Davis, whose roles occupy a fabulous continuum from heroine to villainess. What matters is which one you choose to be, based on limited circumstances and unlimited desires.

Neither performer was known for her comic skills, but over time Denise evolved her own comic set piece. Whenever a white department store saleswoman failed to give her enough—or enough respectful—attention, she would pause, draw herself up, ask: "Do you know who I am?" and in the silence that followed declare: "I'm Martha Graham."

"What did the women say?" I asked when I first heard this story. Denise's response was breezy. "If she was too young or ignorant to know who Graham was, she'd get sheepish or decide I was crazy. Either way she gave me what I wanted as quickly and humbly as possible. If she knew who Graham was, she'd try to hide her double take, then give a feeble 'Oh' or a respectful, noncommittal 'That's incredible.' Then I'd relent and give her my imperious smile. When Diahann Carroll was on *Dynasty* I'd use her sometimes. Then the woman would gush, address me as Dominique Devereaux and beg me to take all their most expensive cosmetic samples."

I've spent my adult years working on an assemblage of black feminist anger modes. My sources vary. And I don't hesitate to draw from non-black styles when they have something vibrant to offer.

By the '70s Nina Simone was an oracle of black power, of our collective grief and fury. "Four Women." "Mississippi Goddam." "Backlash Blues." "I Wish I Knew How It Would Feel to Be Free." I was worshipful, but from a distance. And I couldn't really see beyond the epic race rage to the internal anguish, the breakdowns she was enduring. Which I would have felt more temperamental kinship with. When you're bipolar, one part of you is always staging a backlash against the other. Assault, assuage. Conquer, cower. Back and forth, back and forth. This was too painful, maybe too shameful to be part of the official Nina Simone discourse. We saw only the public explosions and we cowered before them. Like when she banged the keys, slammed the piano shut and stormed offstage after someone asked her to sing "I Loves You, Porgy." Like when she canceled performance after performance as you stood in line with your ticket.

I looked elsewhere. I wanted violence that was in total control of its effects and victories. That could be antic. Insurgent funk diva Betty Davis on the cover of *They Say I'm Different,* in her space warrior corset and marabou-trimmed boots, crouched in a pre-attack stance, holding a bow-like weapon in each manicured hand; her Afro a burning bush, her face serenely confident. Betty Davis on "Nasty Gal," growling screaming, exalting: "You said I was a witch now / You said I was a bitch now / I'm gonna tell 'em why." Grinding, kicking, thrusting and strutting. Sex as jubilant terrorism.

At the other end of the content spectrum but with the same consummate performative violence was Valerie Solanas's *SCUM Manifesto,* with its full-blast contempt for a hetero-patriarchy, which "if the bomb doesn't drop on it will hump itself to death . . . If SCUM ever marches, it will be over the President's stupid, sickening face. If SCUM ever strikes, it will be in the dark with a six-inch blade."

I also treasured the small, concentrated dose of disdain or anger: the line that, like a syringe, aimed, pierced, injected its poison and briskly withdrew. As when Ti-Grace Atkinson shut down a marriage proposal with "I can't marry you, Archie. I have no money and you have no character."

As when Ethel Waters observed, after reading a news item about a woman who'd shot her lover:

"She shot him lightly and he died politely."

These last examples gesture toward a mode I want to work with more, where anger uses comic brevity and takes pleasure in taut prosody. I call it the counter-diva mode.

But I still cherish the grand exit. And after all these years, my favorite is still the one I learned in childhood from the Grimms' fairy tale "Rumpelstiltskin."

I deliver my lines. Then I turn, wheel, kick, stomp my foot; disappear into the earth that has groaned and rumbled open to welcome me.

VII

Why let this nasty dwarf intrude on my tribute to virtuosic female anger? I've always felt a kinship with nonhuman creatures driven by desire and unimpeded by doubt. Actual humans who can do this astound me. How could we belong to the same species?, I ask myself. The same race? The same gender?

My mother told me about Josephine Baker in 1963. She was on national television, a legend who'd traveled from France to join Martin Luther King, Jr.'s soon-to-be-legendary March on Washington. Mother described how she'd fought in the 1950s, staged public battles against segregation in Miami theaters and New York nightclubs. And I was impressed. But what clearly excited us both just as much was Baker's (La Bakair's) life as an enchantress in Paris, a dancer, singer and actress who conquered all of Europe and South America with her art. A virtuoso of blazing entrances and exits.

Shaping the world to her will. Here is Josephine Baker, virtuoso of blazing entrances and exits, shaping the world's desires to her will. The diva as imperious sovereign and cocky rebel. The counter-diva as comedienne, hoyden, flirt. The ugly stuff of her life—poverty, neglect, abuse, child labor—was turned onstage into comic peril and triumph. Offstage it became a melodrama in which she could play the menaced heroine and the valorous hero.

She made herself ubiquitous. She made herself immortal.

She said: **"It is the intelligence of my body that I have exploited."** "Exploit" has the same root as "explicate," meaning "to unfold." She trained her body to unfold as **one flawless unit of flesh, muscle, limb, bone and joint**. Colette, a provincial turned Parisian like Josephine, and the great-great-granddaughter of a quadroon (which by the race laws of the United States would have made her a Negro writer), itemized and extolled her oval knees, the ankles that **"flower from the clear, beautiful, even-textured brown skin . . . the hard work of company rehearsals . . . the years and coaching,"** all of which had **"perfected an elongated and discreet bone-structure and retained the admirable convexity of her thighs. Josephine's shoulder-blades are unobtrusive, her shoulders light, she has the belly of a young girl with a high-placed navel . . . Her huge eyes, outlined**

in black and blue, gaze forth, her cheeks are flushed, the moist and dazzling sweetness of her teeth shows between dark and violet lips . . .”

Wherever she was, wherever she went, Josephine was a foreign body; she never belonged fully to anybody or any body politic. And in a world where black culture was so often deemed a threat to, even a crime against, Western civilization, Josephine Baker was the body of the offense.

Now, think of the soul as the body's twin: its animating breath and spirit—*le gros bon ange* at the crossroads of all civilizations. Think of Josephine as the Psyche who chose to be chosen by Eros. She was always envisioning a spectacular future: for herself first; for the whole world eventually.

“Originality is the modification of ideas,” and this woman never met an idea she couldn't modify. **Civilization is the exchange of ideas between groups. While she lived and moved in the midst of a white civilization, everything that she touched was re-interpreted for her own use.** She was a theater star who aroused the fantasies and anxieties of millions. She turned herself into a political visionary who longed to embody the hopes of millions.

Josephine Baker produced three autobiographies—just like Frederick Douglass. When she wrote a novel, she took Pauline Hopkins's daring title, *Of One Blood,* one step beyond: she called it *My Blood in Your Veins.* **A great performer is an author who writes a book each night onstage.** Josephine was a great performer. And a performer's body, like a writer's book, absorbs influences and traditions. Josephine's body absorbed her predecessors'.

Great soloists never perform entirely alone. They always contain allusions to unseen bodies. We know so little about Josephine's predecessors. Alice Whitman, "Queen of the Tappers," who could Shim Sham Shimmy, "mostly from the waist down," dimpled kneecaps quivering all the while. Ida Forsyne, with her Russian folk dance and her ragtime toe dance. ("Go on, Ida, show 'em!" Bessie Smith shouted from the wings.) Ethel Williams, hurling her limbs into the Texas Tommy, and balling the jack while she circle-danced.

Ma Rainey sang, "All the boys in the neighborhood / They say your Black Bottom is really good." Ethel Waters sang, "Now, it ain't no Charleston, ain't no Pigeon Wing / Nobody has to give you no lessons to shake that thing . . ." Bessie Smith and Alberta Hunter sang, "Strut your stuff / Strut your stuff! / Cake Walking Babies from Home!"

Josephine Baker was the first black woman to give these *dances* star status. And though she had partners for some numbers, she was, above all, a soloist. (Her white predecessors and peers Irene Castle and Adele Astaire were celebrated as partners and both retired young. Her great black predecessor, Florence Mills, died young.) Night after night, year after year, there she was, in New York, Paris, Berlin, Buenos Aires: syncopating, demonstrating; cakewalking in pointe shoes and plumed tail feathers; swinging-step into a Paris dive to show off her black bottom, her hoofing and her ballet girl chainé turns. You feel the pleasure of weight released in her Charleston; her legs follow a slight curve upwards—you can see the thigh muscles powering her—and her arms rotate through the air as if it were slightly resistant, slightly buoyant like water. Improvisation, composition, signature moves and the vamping—ready shtick that keeps an audience happy till you're willing to give them something more.

She was born between two generations of great black women performers: Bessie Smith, Clara Smith and Ethel Waters on one side; Ella Fitzgerald, Billie Holiday and Sarah Vaughan on the other. And those elusive theater legends in black and white: Florence Mills and Adele Astaire. Mills caught the melancholy that shadowed Harlem merriment ("I'm a little blackbird **looking for a bluebird**"); Astaire caught the hedonism of Nordic smart set niceties. Josephine found a use for both: she played the merry soubrette, the lyric ingenue, the top hat, white tie and tails dandy. Listen to her voice as it develops, floating and skipping along on high notes, doll's house thin and garish-bright at first, then morphing into a silk-light conduit for operetta ornament, a plush diseuse of jazz intonations and inflections. One needs many tongues to speak of Baker. **One needs a hundred pairs of eyes to get 'round this woman**.

Sing and dance, Josephine**. Excite, incite,** pose and promenade. She was notorious for exposing her body, minimally embellished with pearls, or bananas. "Exposed" has the same root as "expound," meaning to set out, to place with great care.

Her head, that brown egg of a head, was often the most heavily costumed portion of her body: first there was the cap of hair and the art deco forehead curl, later there was the high, thick, swinging ponytail and headdresses elaborate as palace gates. Explicate, unfold, expound; set out and place. All of this will be done with the map of Josephine's body: it will become **"a mobile army of metaphors"** calling up Africa, the Caribbean, America and Europe; playing on the borders between modernism and primitivism, between high and popular art, civilization and savagery. It will be a valuable, one-of-a-kind symbol of the global art traffic in black bodies and souls.

Josephine Baker was at the center of modernism's drive to colonize Negro creativity and to police Negro art. The intellectuals and journalists at the center of this drive reasoned it this way: there were resources a-plenty in this Negro stuff, but **"the nigger sculpture,"** the sounds of **"the nigger bands"** that found a way into the work of so many white artists, were the crude material of art: the Negro didn't understand how to give it significant lasting form. And if, occasionally, it looked as if a few Negroes had given the stuff significant lasting form, that was a happy accident. They didn't know they were doing it. When they made a conscious attempt to create serious art, they resorted to mimicry—naïve and grandiose mimicry. **"Too much 'art' and not enough Africa"** was a typical verdict. Artlessness was the Negro's only shot at art.

This ideology ruled Josephine Baker's films. The French imagination had no interest in a character who was not a pure-in-heart primitive from a distant land familiarized as a former colony. She made three movies, and each one took the story of her rise from obscurity to celebrity and wrapped it in a see-through layer of colonial fantasy. No St. Louis, no Harlem. No forebears (though *Zouzou* harks back to Columbus's belief that he'd discovered India: her French guardian says she was born in Polynesia of Chinese-Indian parents). Josephine's character always starts out as a merry peasant or laundress. Then, through a set of accidents and the ploys of some canny Frenchman, she becomes the toast of Paris. In the end, she returns to happy tropical obscurity or languishes in the gilded cage of stardom. No film allowed Josephine to glorify her rise, her conquests, her role as a cultural buccaneer—as decades older, white Mae West did over and over. These are Cinderella stories that end sadly-ever-after because this Cinderella can never scrub the dirt off her face. A white prince marries a white princess. Race royals must mate. French audiences had to be carefully taught that this superstar, hailing from a country more powerful than theirs, appearing in their most glamorous theaters, speaking their language, wearing their best clothes, collecting European lovers, was actually a permanent citizen of a land called "Their Basic Black Savagery." There, talent and craft are happy pre-conscious accidents. There, humor is always broad and often grotesque. There, sensuality is never far from the bestial.

Watch the scene in *Princess Tam-Tam,* where Josephine abandons herself to the call of the drums in a chic Parisian ballroom. **What is Africa to me?** When she dances it is the well-placed pelvic throb, legs apart, feet rooted, thigh muscles doing their work for all to see; the face—a series of quick-change masks, each signaling **ferocious abandon**. We watch the faces of the jaded French sophisticates: shock, embarrassment, disdain. We are being asked to do the impossible: to live inside those reactions and to vault past them—for Josephine is a star, the creature of desire—to live out her virtuosic abandon, yet patronize it. I can't outwit this scene. It contains too many treacheries.

So let's turn away from that, and regard Josephine Baker as a New Negro and a New Woman. *The New Negro:* independent-thinking, international, in the advance guard of the African diaspora, **scaling the racial mountain, expressing her individual dark-skinned self without fear or shame**, inventing new characteristics of Negro Expression every day.

Dynamic suggestion. Ferocious abandon. The rhythm of segments. Tropic nonchalance.

The New Woman: determined to exercise her mind and her talents fully, to effect change in society; ready to **"experiment with herself, to capitalize her natural resources and get her money's worth . . . to apply business methods to being young."**

And then there is the *New Negro Woman,* still compromised by, still compensating for (and compensation is a form of penance), her sexually-defiled-beast-of-labor past: **"She is conscious that what is left of chivalry is not directed toward her. She realizes that the ideals of beauty, built up in the fine arts, have excluded her almost entirely."**

Josephine vaulted past being a good girl and a lady. She

made herself a global New Negro Woman—a woman of means, a woman of fashion and of appetites, artist and muse, most faithful to herself. Writing her books onstage night after night, collaborating with ghostwriters, improvising with reporters, to document her life and self.

You have been called pre-human, Miss Baker, a monkey, a leopard, a sign that man is reverting to the apes. **"People have done me the honor of comparing me to an animal."**

Your masculine admirers are legion, Miss Baker. Who do you love? **"I love wives of gentlemen because it is frightening to think that without them I would be alone with all the men on earth."**

How many years after emancipation did race men and women bemoan the shame of the Negro woman, lament the caste restrictions of femininity? **(A Negro woman cannot be a lady.)** A Negro woman must never cease to fight **"poverty, proscription and prejudice,"** alongside the Negro man, but in her own particular sphere she must labor to **uphold purity, honor chastity and rebut derision.**

Go back to a scene from the eighteenth century. **"Visiting the slave market in Boston one day in 1761, Mrs.**

John Wheatley was attracted by the modest demeanor and intelligent countenance of a delicate-looking black girl just from the slave ship. She was quite nude save for a piece of coarse carpet she had tied around her loins."

What fascinates here is the glimpse of the naked girl who would become Phillis Wheatley, the founding mother of poetry and propriety in Negro literature. (And isn't propriety a form of dress?) There's a touch of the artist too, in that piece of carpet. And this little domestic slave girl would soon be reading—English first, then Greek and Latin—and deftly mimicking eighteenth-century prosody; publishing, traveling to England, meeting George Washington.

We use what we've got to get what we want. This little domestic serving girl, Josephine of East St. Louis, found her way past poverty, propriety and proscription to do just that.

She mimicked every performer she saw who had something worth mimicking. Then she ran it through **"the alembic of her genius."** She can make ugly beauty out of minstrel antics (the eyes roll, the mouth spreads in a half-moon demon child grin; the feathered rump thrusts up decisively and out derisively). She can do Femme Glamour, Drag King top-hat-and-tails chic, showgirl élan.

She can even do modesty. **"Josephine naked will teach other performers the meaning of modesty,"** said Colette. Her body was her armor when she went naked.

That body had been a tool of labor when she worked as a maid; it would remain a tool, an instrument to be labored over. But like so many black women who left domestic work for show business in those years, she learned to labor with her mind and soul, too. **"She could dance and she could clown joy into you. And she could also play the trombone,"** said Ethel Waters. She labored to produce joy. And to experience it.

Baker, exuberantly, played the muse to artists. The Le Corbusier designs for her chateau; the drawings, posters and stage sets of Covarrubias and Colin; the wire sculptures of Calder; the designs of Poiret and Balenciaga; the way Balanchine coded her body into his jazz ballet aesthetic. In 2006, the classical quintet Imani Winds created a full-length multi-media called *Josephine Baker: A Life of le Jazz Hot!* In 2019 Tyshawn Sorey and Claudia Rankine created *Perle Noir: Meditations for Josephine,* a music theater piece performed by the soprano Julia Bullock.

She was her own devoted muse. She made her life a spectacular traveling production; she found new roles and plotlines for herself (military spy, political activist, global mother); she rotated leading men; she hired, fired and mentored supporting players. Look at her life and you'll find a web of tropes and symbols. Here are a few of my favorites.

—Josephine's childhood nickname was Tumpy, **"because I was as fat as Humpty Dumpty,"** she claimed. Who learned better than she the lesson Humpty Dumpty forced upon Alice: that words can mean whatever you want them to mean? Deeds, too. **"The question is: who is to be master?"**

—Josephine gladly fled America for Europe in 1925. When she returned in 1937 to star in *The Ziegfeld Follies,* one critic sniffily called her **"the most prominent Negress since Eliza in *Uncle Tom's Cabin.*"** Well, her life *was* a series of flights. She fled toil, fitful maternal care, sexual bargains struck too often and marriages made too soon. In 1917, she had seen the burning houses of blacks as they fled the murderous white mobs of East St. Louis. Forever after she swore it was not the houses she saw, but the people. **"I see them running, to get to the bridge," she insisted. "I have been running ever since."** Running toward safety, toward pleasure, toward glory.

—For her first lead role on Broadway she played Topsy Anna in Noble Sissle and Eubie Blake's *The Chocolate Dandies.* She and Sissle gave Topsy a black face and white lips (from whence came the sounds of a muted saxophone). A mammy-made checked dress and frog-feet clown shoes. As Anna she displayed a smart, flapper bob, a gold lamé gown with dyed-to-match shoes, and the prettily angled leg and clasped hands of a hostess about to favor her guests with a drawing room ballad. Like Topsy, she sang, danced and clowned. And she didn't have to renounce her wicked ways for religion and missionary work.

—Josephine got her break from black men who infiltrated the musical theater in 1921. But she got her start from the blues women who came to power in 1920. She was taken up by the Queen of the Moaners, Clara Smith. She learned plenty about performing, and in her own way she learned the blues singer's trick of revising shared material to suit herself. Clara sang "Freight Train Blues" with the lines **"When a woman gets the blues she goes to her room and cries / But when a man gets the blues he catches a freight train and rides."** Josephine never sang or lived the blues; she found her own way to upend them. She found the will and the means to catch a train, plane or transatlantic liner and ride.

—How does it feel to spend a big chunk of your celebrated life feeling that you're not black enough for blacks or white enough for whites? **"How does it feel to be a problem?"** Double consciousness is a triple burden for performers: How do they live except by seeing themselves through the eyes of their audience and manipulating what the audience sees at the same time? Ruling and subjecting yourself time after time.

Do people of color today still have dual personalities, one for whites, one disclosed **"only in the freemasonry of the race"**? Josephine's personality shifts were dictated by ego, circumstance, instinct, conviction and strategy. I'd say she foreshadowed how we live here and now. We know, we declare vehemently that race is a construction. We also know that race is a construction site we're not going to be leaving any time soon. There was Josephine with her negligent black mother and her missing, most-likely-white father; Josephine, mocked as "chocolate" and "pinky" by neighbors; Josephine, living in and with multiple languages all at once. What are we to do with her—*and our*—multiple selves, conjoined here, cross-wired there?

Like the rest of us, she sustained damage. Yes, she straightened her hair so much that she burned her head bare; yes, she longed to marry a well-born, well-to-do white man, and she never managed to; yes, her vanity and touchiness could undercut her generosity and her bravery. As could the racial insults that lurked in Europe and attacked in the States.

It's excruciating to read about her *Ziegfeld Follies of 1937* experience. She was treated like a second-string performer, not a headliner, and, except for a Balanchine number, she was given second-rate material. The show business version of second-class citizenship. The reviewers gloated as they dismissed and belittled her. She was not supposed to act like an international star and a citizen of France, she was supposed to act like a lower-caste American Negro grateful to be home again. She was furious, she was traumatized, she fought back. She struck out, too, and when that happened, it wasn't just white people who felt the blows.

She would not give interviews to black newspapers. She would speak only French at a Harlem party given in her honor. If you were a black friend from the old days, you might find yourself snubbed. If you were a white journalist asking about the old days, you might be informed that she was Spanish on her father's side and on her mother's half-Indian, "half-colored." One of the stories that buzzed through Harlem had Ethel Waters coming to pay La Bakair her "professional respects" and getting snubbed. But let me say this about Ethel Waters: between 1933 and 1936, she triumphed with parodies of Josephine in not one but two Broadway productions. In *At Home Abroad* she played the swell-headed *Hottentot Potentate,* courtesy of Howard Dietz and Arthur Schwartz. In *As Thousands*

Cheer she played Irving Berlin's little colored girl, lost in the wiles of Paris, denied her right to be lowdown, and confessing:

> My parlez-vous will not ring true
> With Harlem on my mind.

It was grueling, this American experience. It shocked her. But at least it helped ready her for what would be her next role in the theaters of war and race struggle.

1943: Black U.S. Army troops in Morocco are denied the chance to fight and confined to the segregated Liberty service club. Baker wows them: she gives them entertainment, she gives them uplift, she promises to come back to the States when the war is won and join the fight against segregation.

1950: She comes back to the U.S. and promptly breaks the color bar at a swank Miami nightclub. She gives interviews to black newspapers; she plays black theaters. She does her own version of a civil rights prizefight, head-to-head with the Stork Club, with Walter Winchell and with the Hearst Corporation. Called a crypto-Communist fellow-traveler; her FBI file also notes that (1) she had said she hated the United States; (2) she would do anything to further her career (surely a trait she shared with J. Edgar Hoover); and (3) she had, as a young woman in

France, **"been promiscuous in her sexual relations with both men and women."**

I get tired of thinking of women like Baker as traditional divas. We marvel at diva gifts; we ogle and patronize diva excess. But goddesses belong to myth, not history, and in their legendary fits of rage and destruction they can remind me more of early models for female "hysterics" than female artists. The greats we call divas, women like Baker, Ethel Waters, Bessie Smith, like Isadora Duncan and Martha Graham, are as much combatants and liberators as they are divas.

Watch: Josephine Baker is being rewarded for her World War II service by General De Gaulle. What a coup—acting like Harriet Tubman in her war spy days while looking like Mata Hari in her glory days. Watch: Josephine Baker raises money for Castro and the Cuban Revolution. Watch: Baker accepts Martin Luther King's thanks for her work in the Civil Rights Movement.

I think Baker played the wanton, selfish goddess most when she played The Mother. Her body could not conceive children. But she wanted to create a new race, so she did what gods and goddesses and child-bearing women do; she used the human material at hand. She found children in poor families and in orphanages; she took them and set out to mold them into a Rainbow Tribe, a universal family that would refute racism . . . and embody "ma vie en toutes les couleurs." Her rule was absolute: gods and goddesses set the terms for human survival. I am your destiny. You must take my love on faith. In return I will care for you. However I choose to act, you will honor, obey and worship me.

Isn't it interesting that, having *shown* herself to all kinds of people, she began to *speak* for all people? Envisioned for so long, she chose to become a visionary. She said: **"Surely the day will come when color means nothing more than the skin tone, when religion is seen uniquely as a way to speak one's soul; when birth places have the weight of a throw of the dice and all men are born free, when understanding breeds love and brotherhood."**

What tickles me is that inside this oratory, with its slightly too opulent grandeur, I hear a trouper working changes on familiar material and coming up with something fresh for her audience. Color is no longer the cursed mark of caste, it is a matter of individual palettes and natural aesthetic selection. Religion is not proscriptive doctrine; it is a form of self-expression, like art. The land of one's birth does not define one's social or political destiny. Destiny becomes a game of chance, guided by skill and talent.

And finally we come to that well-worn rhetorical trio: love, brotherhood and understanding. She doesn't start with love, as so many orators still do—she knows that love without "understanding" is careless, reckless love. She knows that understanding comes from unending hard work, and that without some infusion of love it can stall at anger and despair. As for brotherhood . . . well, like **"all men,"** its limits are glaringly clear: how nice that it comes last. Can any of us fully escape the language of our age? In that age, everyone knew that only women who'd already claimed male prerogatives dared claim the kind of lofty male language that pretended to be universal. She lived as though it were.

That's why I cherish her honorable, tactically brilliant appearance at the 1963 March on Washington.

She arrived wearing the uniform of the Free French Army and the implacably big, implacably black sunglasses of the female star *d'un certain age.*

She was the only woman permitted to speak on the program.

She had placed herself beyond gender and genre judgments.

She was the only decorated war hero in view.

. . .

Josephine Baker had one of those natures made for victory. Will and desire were conjoined. Her eyes saw a horizon where adversity yielded to conquest, to abundant pleasures and possibilities.

I marvel at people like this. They refuse to be impeded by terror, doubt and a kind of fury that shuts the self down and then shuts the world out. They aren't like me. And that can make me feel like Dr. Frankenstein's monster, lamenting his alienation from humans. "Shall I respect man when he contemns me? Let him live with me in the interchange of kindness, and, instead of injury, I would bestow every benefit upon him with tears of gratitude and acceptance. But that cannot be; the human senses are insurmountable barriers to our union."

I love those last mournful words. They're worth wallowing in (and I wallow, I admit). But it's not the human senses that set me apart from others, it's the human psyche. Or it's my kind of psyche, which insists on feeling most itself when in pain.

. . .

. . . People do everything . . .
All those odd things that they do,
Like falling in love with shoes and
Sewing buttons on themselves

And hearing voices, and thinking themselves
Napoleon.
are natural:
Have a place.
Madness and aberration are not only part of the
whole tremendous setup,
but also (I have come to believe) important
parts. Life
trying new ways
out
and around
and through.

These words never fail to move me. Louise Bogan wrote them in 1939, and for the thirty years that followed she kept on writing poetry, she kept on writing criticism, she kept having and recovering from nervous breakdowns. So I hear her valor, her refusal of waste. (She was good at refusal—of one breakdown she wrote: "I refused to fall apart, so I have been taken apart, like a watch.")

Then, once I've basked in being moved by Bogan, something deflates me. Is it the hint of theatricality, of valor so effectively backlit? When the sentence ends, isn't daily life right there again, saying flatly: stop piercing your skin, sew the damned buttons back on your clothes and put the shoes you've been fondling back in the closet. Or you'll pay. And pay. And pay.

Is there a note of spite in my rejoinder? What provoked it? I'm not sure. Was it a sudden recollection that Bogan, wounded for life by her working-class Irish origins, had still referred dismissively in a letter to "the dark Miss [Gwendolyn] Brooks, with poems on roaches, dead white men, etc." Is this a memory that's with me always? No. It's one that vanishes for long periods of time, then gets pushed to the surface by the pressure of some other memory.

In the 1970s—nearly forty years after Louise Bogan wrote these words—Irma Jefferson and four of her Birthday Club chums were lunching contentedly at a Chicago restaurant. As they began dessert, a frail, sallow woman approached their table and stood waiting till they grew silent. Then she introduced herself with the words, *"None of you recognizes me, do you?"* No, the Birthday Club members did not recognize her; they had raised their eyebrows as in "*what* and *who* is this?" when she arrived at their table. Then the frail, sallow revenant spoke her name—"I'm Janice Kingslow"—and watched as they were gripped and shaken by memories of the vibrant, young Negro actress, a sorority sister they'd been proud to know and champion, for she'd starred in that acclaimed 1940s Negro drama, *Anna Lucasta,* playing a preacher's daughter who rebels against her upright father and stumbles into prostitution; then, having high rather than wanton spirits and wanting a better life, returns home, rejects her sailor lover and finds the sanctity of marriage with an upstanding college graduate. Janice Kingslow starred in the Chicago production and then on Broadway; Hollywood came calling after that, but she refused its blandishments when the contract stipulated that she must change her name and her race, become a white actress (of Mediterranean extraction if asked). No, she'd written "I Refuse to Pass" for the *Negro Digest,* and returned to Chicago to co-found the DuBois Players, a progressive Negro theater company and perform in progressive radio shows like *Destination Freedom* and *Democracy Now!* while advising station executives on how to improve scripts and roles for Negro actors. (Advice politely received and firmly ignored.) Things had begun to curdle some time after that, and by the mid-'50s Janice Kingslow had all but disappeared.

Until the September 1959 issue of *Ebony* magazine, where her first-person essay appeared, titled "TRAPPED BETWEEN TWO WORLDS: A woman's dramatic report of her fight for sanity in a world of pressures and prejudices." There, Kingslow revealed that for the last four years she had "been living in the unreal world of the mentally ill."

The cause? A series of blows, personal and professional, racial and sexual: "too much emotional trauma, frustration and insecurity; too light-skinned to play recognizably Negro characters; too publicly known as a Negro to play white characters or Negro characters who passed for white." Serious love affairs gone smash; even the work she did get (Encyclopaedia Britannica educational films) threatened when she was blacklisted for signing "leftist/communist" petitions and working in "leftist" pro-civil-rights radio dramas. Paranoia, panic, self-loathing, delusions of grandeur overwhelmed her. The day a roommate found her huddled outside their apartment too afraid to go in was the day she first entered a mental institution. In *Ebony,* she wrote:

> For the last two years my home has been a ward in a state mental hospital. Music from a radio softens the physical starkness of the ward. A few yards away paces a patient muttering endlessly against imagined indignities. Down the corridor another sits motionless and withdrawn. At the far end of the building, a woman broken in mind and body refuses to accept the food that will preserve what last vestige of life is

left within her. Nearby a patient sits reading quietly and still another crochets.

In lighter moments, patients would share a laugh at the widely circulated joke which had them quarreling over who among them was *really* Napoleon.

1959. *Ebony* must have required and Kingslow must have desired a story that arced toward healing (and, bless her heart, included a plea for more enlightened treatment of the mentally ill). In the photo at the top of the story, Kingslow sits on her hospital bed in nightclothes, hands folded, eyes staring straight ahead; in the closing photo she walks purposefully, en route to a weekend visit with friends, looking smart in a black skirt and white shirt.

Irma and her friends might well have read this. But Irma and her friends had lost touch with her by then.

The trail I'm pursuing goes cold until 1963, when one Mary Webb writes *Negro Digest* to ask: "Whatever happened to Janice Kingslow?" The "Who and Where Are They" column does a one-sentence recap of her theater and radio work and seals it closed with the words "In recent years she has been inactive in public life."

Now, in the 1970s, as Janice Kingslow stood at the Birthday Club table, the celebrants recalled that she was a good five years younger than they. (How proud of their little Delta pledgee they'd been.) Now they were in their fifties and sixties, while she looked at least five years older—no cosmetics had shielded her skin's decay, no hairdresser had tended the once-lustrous hair now gathered dully at the nape of her neck.

You don't recognize me, do you? I'm Janice Kingslow. Telling me the story not long after, my mother ended it with these words:

I hate waste.

For it *was* waste. What my mother did not say was that during the blacklist days, Janice had been working as the public relations director at Provident Hospital for several years. It was a job she loved—and a job she was "let go" from, suddenly and without explanation, during the blacklist days. I do a quick calculation and I'm stricken. My father would have been the head of Pediatrics at Provident. Did he protest or did he go along with this craven expediency? Did he discuss it with my mother? What advice did she offer? Was she thinking of this when she spoke of hating *waste* with such vehemence?

Janice Kingslow still remains obscure. No longer erased: a small cluster of writers, educators and scholars (of theater, of racial passing and skin color parsing, of black Chicago's Arts and Culture Movements) have included materials on her in their archives at the Vivian G. Harsh Research Collection of Afro-American History at the Carter G. Woodson Branch of the Chicago Public Library. Now she can be referred to with the formal if periodic respect we give compelling, cautionary minor figures—so often women—who lost their place in whatever firmament had briefly exalted them.

Her valiant efforts to shape a life with meaning, her frayed and bifurcated psyche—these can be honorably reframed as "life trying new ways out and through" especially for younger actresses of color, for Black, Indigenous, Latinx and Asian actresses with pale complexions and features that read as ethnically ambiguous. Unsettling. These younger performers can herald her efforts, her courage in refusing to renounce her race, they can speak of standing on her shoulders as they seek and find opportunities—to act, to direct, to produce—that she could only dream of or rebuke herself for dreaming of.

This honorable commentary: does it redeem a life that succumbed to paranoia, panic and self-loathing then wasted away from grief, rage and despair? How Irma Jefferson feared and hated this waste of resources on a black, female terrain where resources were so regularly dismissed or violated. She and her friends had been carefully taught to succeed as women of the black haute bourgeoisie were supposed to succeed. To excel at their profession or professions (wife, mother, socialite, social worker, teacher, lawyer, doctor, businesswoman). To impart ambition and character to the children in their care. To set a good example for their community. To be part of a Negro life and history that moved forward and upward toward justice and victory. Historical and personal loss merged comprehensively for Janice Kingslow. For those who've come after, History keeps trying new ways out and around and through. Black history, women's history, black women's history.

But at that time, in that place, what called itself American History could not be bothered with her.

VIII

Josephine Baker had one of those natures made for victory.

Janice Kingslow did not.

My grandmothers—both of them—had natures made for victory. Opportunity was to be sensed and seized on. Adversity would eventually yield some kind of victory. At times I've feared that if I hadn't been born just as the twentieth century was staggering toward the redemptive tumult of the '50s and '60s, I would have slid (oh so passively, so resentfully) into an expedient marriage, a respectably uninspiring job and year after year of Valium and liquor, managed discreetly enough to keep me from being a social embarrassment. My grandmothers would have tolerated the surface of that life and disdained the subtext.

So when you enter a black narrative, note the figure of the black grandmother. Look, there she is. Defining legacies. Interpreting, if need be inventing, traditions.

Black grandmother figures are resourceful. Proudly unsentimental. The black grandmother embodies endurance, and "endurance" always means the forced shouldering of heavy loads; a life spent paying American society a debt you never owed. Even if that grandmother flourished during all the years you knew her, even if she had little interest in sharing harsh memories, she embodied what must be done to succeed in a world that was at best indifferent and at worst unjust—relentlessly, doggedly unjust.

You do not stop working to live up to your grandmothers. Your task is to justify their accomplishments by exceeding them. To excel at what they approved of.

You revere them. You cower before them. All those proud, eager words about your nervous system? Reverence can make a nervous system experience numbness, episodes of memory loss and blurry vision.

I went to many feminist meetings in the seventies. Black, white, radical, mainstream, thrilling, dutiful. All of them obsessed with our histories and legacies—political, ethical, emotional—as women.

The meeting I want to relive here was organized by Black Women for Wages for Housework. Was it at a women's center, at a union hall? The room was full. I remember that. There were seasoned labor organizers and civil rights veterans; women in their forties, fifties and sixties. There were black feminists and students; there were so-called young professionals like me, in our twenties and thirties, who'd benefitted (I should say profited) from each and every demand, each and every advance in Civil Rights, Black Power, Power, Feminism and Gay Rights. The meeting began with formal presentations; it moved into spontaneous declarations. I was sitting near an attractive black woman about my age. She could have been a writer or artist; she could have been a graduate student: she looked too bohemian to be a lawyer or doctor, but of course this was a weekend and a political meeting. Many of us had wardrobes to meet the requirements of midtown offices, downtown readings, late-night clubs and midday demonstrations. I liked how alertly this woman listened, especially to the older, more experienced women. I hoped I mirrored her. I thought I might introduce myself afterwards. So I was pleased when she stood up and passionately seconded everything that had been said about class and income disparities, about centuries of unpaid labor, about making sure that unprotected low-wage domestic workers were not just included but foregrounded in our demands. She looked around the room and paused before offering her final words. "Black women are *tired*," she said, shaking her head and switching from a midtown to a soulful uptown voice.

"***I'm*** tired," she said, and put one hand on her hip.

"I'm tired for what my *grand*mama did."

There were affirmative chuckles, responsive *ummms.* And no sooner had I offered mine than I found myself in a silent rage. *"Oh really? Really? Why don't you let your grandmother be tired for* herself*? Why don't you stop poaching on her history? Why don't you stop flaunting virtues you've only won through family connections?"* I continued this rant in my journal when I got home a few hours later. *It's so American and entitled, this fetish worship of ancestors' loss and deprivation. I'd love to blame it on sentimental white European immigrants who always talk about their people's sufferings in the old country when the subject is slavery and it's been pointed out that none of their people were enslaved or exterminated here. My generation of black women is doing the same thing. Wearing the garb of ancestral suffering like it was vintage clothing.*

Forty-plus years and many diaries later I reread this. And suddenly the personal springs up scratching and clawing at my critical disdain. A memory exhumes itself, one I'd buried alive and left for dead long ago.

When my Chicago grandmother died, I was nine and I was not at the hospital. I was told her last words were: "I'm so tired. So tired."

She hadn't been tired on all those weekends my sister and I spent at her house: us watching Gorgeous

George and Liberace on television, us watching her play canasta with her friends Jewel and Bessie; us watching as she made our breakfast; us watching her lay out fresh towels and washcloths; us reading in the sunroom while she cooked the thick, heavy bread pudding we loved; me standing very still by her sewing machine as Denise helped her measure the black ruffles that would trim my scarlet sateen Gypsy Halloween skirt.

I don't remember my grandmother seeming tired from the forty years of work she'd done in order to succeed in four professions—dressmaking, politics, real estate, raising an accomplished daughter—all while widowed once, divorced once and married twice; all while advancing North with the Great Migration: Holly Springs, Mississippi, to St. Louis, Missouri, to Chicago, Illinois.

I was taught this narrative when I was in my twenties and old enough to savor the Life and Legend of Lillian McClendon Armstrong Saunders Thompson. Her imperiousness suddenly made more sense: the quick-witted warmth that would turn cold and implacable when my sister and I misbehaved, or when her tenants made excuses for not having the rent. "But, Mrs. Thompson, I don't have—"

"I'm not interested in what you don't have, Mrs. Jackson."

When I was four and running as fast as I could around her living room, I crashed into her favorite lamp. As it lay broken on the floor, I answered her angry outbursts with the words "I'm never coming here again," to which she replied "Good!"—then laughed as I toddled haughtily toward the front door. "Now, Donkey, come back," she said, and broke the curse.

When I was eight and Denise eleven, we decided to talk with Mother about Grandma's disciplinary habits. We *loveherloveherloveher,* we *love* spending time with her, we said, but when we do something she doesn't like she won't even let us try to explain, no matter how polite we are. Mother looked pensive. "I know," she answered. "She was the same way with me. I'll do my best."

I have no memory of the afternoon Denise found Grandma collapsed in the linen closet where she'd gone to get fresh sheets for our bed. "Margo, come here. Grandma's fallen!" Denise called out. "We have to get her back into bed." And the two of us, twelve and nine, got her back into bed and Denise called our parents, who drove over as quickly as they could and took her to the hospital. Denise told me this story at least twenty years later; she thought that at last we'd be sharing this memory. I was astounded, though, and kept asking if she was sure it had happened that way. She was. She assumed we'd never discussed it because it still pained us so. I didn't ask (or if I did I don't remember her answering) whether Grandma had recovered and had her fatal heart attack the next year at sixty-five rather than sixty-four. Was this time the last time we saw her face, heard her voice and touched her body? Denise is dead now too, also at sixty-five. People always said she was the one who'd inherited Grandma's temperament.

In that 1975 (or 6) journal, I ended my silent rant about the proper way to honor and eulogize black grandmothers with these words: *You say you're tired for what your grandmother did? You should be tired because, after all her hard work, if your grandmother were alive she'd probably ask if you'd earned your right to be tired yet.*

In the privacy of my own psyche, I was not willing to give space to the figure of the generically tired Black Grandmother. Mine had worked unceasingly to will herself out of that role. And she had an early death to show for it.

If she were alive, here now with me, what would she say? I think she'd say, quietly and not without tenderness: You haven't earned your right to be tired yet, have you, Donkey?

BLACKOUT

Acknowledgements

This book was inspired [illegible]

the [illegible] dating [illegible]

and influenced me. Thanks [illegible]

my family and friends [illegible]

[illegible] and my [illegible]

[illegible]

Acknowledgments

This book was inspired and driven by the art of others. The scope, the daring and the cost of that art have shaped and influenced me. The book is also driven by the lives of my family and friends, not least that of my niece, Francesca Harper, and my great-niece, Harper Cohen. What would I be without all their sensibilities and their stories?

From start to finish, my agent, Sarah Chalfant, has been wonderfully discerning and supportive. I am very grateful to her. I thank the Wylie Agency staff as well, especially Rebecca Nagel.

All my thanks to friends who read portions of the book, who talked me through portions of the book, and who advise, console and delight me year after year: Wendy Gimbel, Nancy Gist, Christine Carter, Ellen Novack, Adrienne Kennedy, Wendy Walters, Drew Gangolf, Tony Heilbut, Darryl Pinckney, James Fenton, Helen Epstein, Judith Thurman and Phillip Lopate.

I lost a longtime Chicago friend this year in Shawn Kennedy. I'm glad her sister, Royal, is still here to reminisce with.

I deeply appreciate Pantheon's support of my book as it evolved. Lisa Lucas is resourceful and indefatigable. My editor, Maria Goldverg, is an editor for all seasons: astute, engaged and imaginative. My thanks to the design staff and the copy editors for their hard work. And to Erroll McDonald for acquiring the book.

Here's to Alicia Archer and Rhiona O'Laughlin for understanding what bodies need to do to do their best work.

Jo Lang understands the complicated ways by which the mind and heart learn to thrive. I honor her. Jean-Pierre Lindenmayer understands too. I thank him.

And, of course, I thank the two cherished friends to whom this book is dedicated.

Notes

I

5 "and just naming names": Gertrude Stein, "Poetry and Grammar," in *Lectures in America* (Beacon Press, 1985), p. 210.

5 "as if the top of your head": Emily Dickinson, *Selected Letters,* ed. Thomas H. Johnson (Belknap Press/Harvard University Press, 1986), p. 208.

9 "unromantic as Monday morning": Charlotte Brontë, *Shirley, A Tale* (1849), chap. 1.

11 "Always in every family": Katherine Anne Porter, "Reflections on Willa Cather," in *The Collected Essays and Occasional Writings of Katherine Anne Porter* (Houghton Mifflin, 1990), p. 32.

16 "True to oneself!": Katherine Mansfield, *The Critical Writings of Katherine Mansfield,* ed. Clare Hanson (Macmillan, 1987), p. 38.

20 *We loved them for the dangers:* After Shakespeare, *Othello,* Pelican Shakespeare (Penguin Books, 1958), pp. 38, 47.

23 *between 1880 and 1930:* Crystal N. Feimster, *Southern Horrors: The Politics of Rape and Lynching* (Harvard University Press, 2009).

II

30 *"If it were possible":* Ida B. Wells, quoted in *We Are Your Sisters: Black Women in the Nineteenth Century,* ed. Dorothy Sterling (W. W. Norton, 1997), p. 493.

34 *"Sometimes it is better to be":* Czeslaw Milosz, quoted in Cynthia

Haven, "Happy Birthday, Czeslaw Milosz!," *The Book Haven* (blog), bookhaven.stanford.edu, June 30, 2016.

36 "Work and sweat": Zora Neale Hurston, "Sweat," in *Hurston: Novels & Stories* (Library of America, 1995), p. 956.

48 "I said, 'A line will take' ": W. B. Yeats, "Adam's Curse," in *The Collected Poems of W. B. Yeats* (Macmillan, 1956), p. 78.

III

56 "a tasteful rhinestone-studded": Jill Watt, *Hattie McDaniel: Black Ambition, White Hollywood* (Amistad, 2007), p. 178.

IV

71 Hawthorne's dark-hued Pearl: *The Scarlet Letter* was published in 1850, the year before *Uncle Tom's Cabin* began appearing in serialized form.

71 "*'How old are you, Topsy?'*": Harriet Beecher Stowe, *The Annotated Uncle Tom's Cabin,* ed. Henry Louis Gates, Jr., and Hollis Roberts (W. W. Norton, 2007), pp. 253–54.

73 "I sometimes wish": Harriet Jacobs, *Incidents in the Life of a Slave Girl,* ed. Jean Fagan Yellin (Harvard University Press, 1987), p. 238.

73 That little Witch Topsy: *Kara Walker: My Complement, My Enemy, My Oppressor, My Love,* Walker Art Center, Minneapolis, 2007.

74 When American horror has invented you: "If Poe were alive, he would not have to invent horror, horror would invent him." Richard Wright, Introduction to *Native Son* (Harper & Row, 1966), p. xxxiv.

74 "Captain Marryat complained": Eugene Genovese, *Roll, Jordan, Roll* (Vintage, 1976), p. 314.

74 "As we crossed Blackwell's Island": F. Scott Fitzgerald, *The Great Gatsby* (Scribner, 1995), p. 73.

82 "I thought God I wonder why": This and all other Tina Turner

quotes are from Tina Turner with Kurt Loder, *I, Tina* (William Morrow, 1986), quoted in Margo Jefferson, "River Deep, Mountain High," *The Nation,* November 1, 1986.

82 *the mere radiance of a foul soul:* Robert Louis Stevenson, *The Strange Case of Dr. Jekyll and Mr. Hyde* (1886; Dover Publications, 1991), p. 10.

97 *she has been severed by: The Story of Mattie L. Jackson: Her Parentage, Experience of Eighteen Years in Slavery; Her Escape from Slavery, Incidents During the War: A True Story* (Oxford University Press, 1988), p. 33; altered.

97 *Wilma, thou shouldst be living:* William Wordsworth, "London, 1802," www.poetryfoundation.org/poems/45528/london-1802; altered.

99 I feel the racial imaginary: *The Racial Imaginary: Writers on Race in the Life of the Mind,* ed. Claudia Rankine and Beth Loffreda (Fence Books, 2015).

100 imagine placing all the techniques: Ellen Novack, *Taming the Cyclops* (Smith and Kraus, 2017), pp. 20, 51.

V

101 Janet Malcolm's theatrically stern words: Janet Malcolm, "Reflections: The Journalist and the Murderer," *The New Yorker,* March 13, 1989, p. 38; altered.

103 as I revised my notes: How many times, to how many classes of impressionable students? I'm writing about delayed recognitions, about evasions and reckonings. My embarrassment can't be purged. So my memory still refuses to be exact.

113 her short 1894 review: Willa Cather, *The World and the Parish: Willa Cather's Articles and Reviews, 1893–1902,* 2 vols., ed. William M. Curtin (University of Nebraska Press, 1970), vol. 1, pp. 165–66. This review seems derived in part from an earlier one by Rebecca Harding Davis. See Daphne Brooks, "'Puzzling the Intervals': Blind Tom and the Poetics of the

Sonic Slave Narrative," in *The Oxford Handbook of the African American Slave Narrative,* Oxford University Press, online edition, May 2014.

119 "spirituals were performed only": Eileen Southern, *The Music of Black Americans: A History* (W. W. Norton, 1997), p. 271.

120 "In the English-horn solo": Alex Ross, "Radical Simplicity," *The New Yorker,* May 31, 2010.

125 I'm bound to question: James Baldwin, "Dialog in Black and White," *Playboy,* December 1966, p. 135.

126 I always go onstage: Sammy Davis, Jr., "*Playboy* Interview: Sammy Davis, Jr.," *Playboy,* December 1966, p. 102.

126 If you can't be free: Adapted from Rita Dove's poem "Canary," used as the title for Farah Jasmine Griffith's book, *If You Can't Be Free, Be a Mystery: In Search of Billie Holiday* (One World, 2002).

VI

138 "Never never will I marry": Frank Loesser, "Never Will I Marry," from the show *Greenwillow,* 1960.

140 Wordsworth's stately formulation: William Wordsworth, "My Heart Leaps Up" (1807).

141 *"What can you say": The Portable Dorothy Parker* (Penguin Books, 1976), pp. 47–48.

VII

151 She made herself ubiquitous: Herman Melville, *Moby-Dick; or, The Whale* (1851; Penguin Books, 1992), p. 197; altered.

151 one flawless unit of flesh: "One flawless unit of fact . . . ," in William James, *The Varieties of Religious Experience* (1902; Modern Library, 1994), p. 149; altered.

151 "flower from the clear": *Josephine Baker,* compilation by Bryan Hammond, biography by Patrick O'Connor (Jonathan Cape, 1988), p. 143.

152 Civilization is the exchange: Zora Neale Hurston, "Characteristics of Negro Expression," in *Hurston: Folklore, Memoirs, & Other Writings* (Library of America, 1995), p. 838; altered.

153 A great performer is an author: Willa Cather, *The Kingdom of Art: Willa Cather's First Principles and Critical Statements, 1893–1896,* ed. Bernice Slote (University of Nebraska Press, 1966), p. 215.

155 One needs a hundred pairs: Virginia Woolf, *To the Lighthouse* (Harcourt, Brace & World, 1955), p. 294; altered.

155 Excite, incite: Nella Larsen, *Quicksand and Passing* (Rutgers University Press, 1986), p. 74; altered.

155 "a mobile army of metaphors": Friedrich Nietzsche, "On Truth and Lies in an Extra-Moral Sense," in *The Portable Nietzsche,* ed. and trans. Walter Kaufmann (Penguin, 1954), pp. 46–47.

156 "the nigger sculpture": Clive Bell, *Since Cézanne* (Harcourt Brace, 1922), p. 121.

156 "the nigger bands": Ibid., p. 218.

156 "Too much 'art' ": Jean-Claude Baker and Chris Chase, *Josephine: The Hungry Heart* (Random House, 1993), p. 74.

157 What is Africa to me?: Countee Cullen, "Heritage," in *The New Negro: Voices of the Harlem Renaissance,* ed. Alain Locke (Atheneum, 1992), p. 250.

157 ferocious abandon: Hurston, "Characteristics of Negro Expression," p. 835.

158 scaling the racial mountain: Langston Hughes, "The Negro Artist and the Racial Mountain," in Arnold Rampersad, *The Life of Langston Hughes, Volume I, 1902–1941: I, Too, Sing America* (Oxford University Press, 1986), pp. 130–31; altered.

158 Dynamic suggestion: Hurston, "Characteristics of Negro Expression," p. 835.

158 Tropic nonchalance: Alain Locke, "Enter the New Negro," in *The New Negro: Voices of the Harlem Renaissance,* ed. Alain Locke (Atheneum, 1992), p. 15.

158 "experiment with herself": Zelda Fitzgerald, "Eulogy on the Flapper," in *Zelda Fitzgerald: The Collected Writings* (Scribner's, 1991), p. 392.

158 "She is conscious that": Elsie McDonald, "The Task of Negro Womanhood," in *The New Negro,* ed. Locke, pp. 369–70.

159 A Negro woman cannot: Anna Julia Cooper, "Womanhood: A Vital Element in the Regeneration and Progress of a Race," in *The Voice of Anna Julia Cooper* (Rowman & Littlefield, 1998), p. 64.

159 "poverty, proscription and prejudice": Frederick Douglass, "To Our Oppressed Countrymen," *The North Star,* December 3, 1847, www.accessible-archives.com.

159 uphold purity, honor chastity: My variation on the "poverty, chastity and derision" theme in Virginia Woolf's *Three Guineas* (Harbinger Books, 1966), p. 79.

159 "Visiting the slave market in Boston": Anna Julia Cooper, "What Are We Worth?," in *The Voice of Anna Julia Cooper,* p. 182.

160 We use what we've got: Lyn Collins, "Think (About It)," 1972, verse 4, Lyrics.com; altered.

160 "the alembic of her genius": James Weldon Johnson, *The Autobiography of an Ex-Coloured Man* (Vintage Books, 1989), p. 100; altered.

161 "Josephine naked will teach": *Josephine Baker,* compilation by Bryan Hammond, biography by Patrick O'Connor, p. 143.

161 "She could dance": Baker and Chase, *Josephine,* p. 28.

162 "The question is": Lewis Carroll, *The Annotated Alice: Alice's Adventures in Wonderland & Through the Looking Glass* (Clarkson N. Potter, 1960), p. 269.

162 "the most prominent Negress": Percy Hammond, *New York Herald Tribune,* quoted in Baker and Chase, *Josephine,* p. 204.

162 "I see them running": Baker and Chase, *Josephine,* p. 30.

163 "How does it feel": W. E. B. Du Bois, *The Souls of Black Folk* (1903; Penguin Classics, 2018), p. 6.

164 "only in the freemasonry": Johnson, *Autobiography of an Ex-Coloured Man,* p. 74.

167 "been promiscuous": Baker and Chase, *Josephine,* p. 310. Baker says he saw the reports; they were supplied by Walter Winchell. The Winchell/Hoover/FBI connection is also discussed, without direct quotes, in Phyllis Rose's *Jazz Cleopatra: Josephine Baker in Her Time* (Doubleday, 1989), pp. 229–30.

168 "Surely the day will come": Blog post on Josephine Baker for Women's History Month 2018, Carolina Women's Center: The Center for Gender Equity, womenscenter.unc.edu/2018/03/whm-josephine-baker/.

170 *". . . People do everything": What the Woman Lived: Selected Letters of Louise Bogan, 1920–1970,* ed. Ruth Limmer (Harcourt Brace Jovanovich, 1973), pp. 181–82. I have recast Bogan's prose as verse.

171 "I refused to fall apart": Ibid., p. 57.

172 "the dark Miss [Gwendolyn] Brooks": Ibid., p. 347.

Permissions Acknowledgments

Grateful acknowledgment is made for permission to reprint the following previously published material:

Hal Leonard: Lyrics to Frank Loesser's "Never Will I Marry" used with permission from Hal Leonard. Copyright © 1960 by Hal Leonard.

Penguin Random House LLC: Lines from Dorothy Parker's poem "Coda" used with permission from Penguin Random House LLC. Copyright © 1928 by Penguin Random House LLC.

A Note on the Type

This book was set in Adobe Garamond. Designed for the Adobe Corporation by Robert Slimbach, the fonts are based on types first cut by Claude Garamond (ca. 1480–1561).